EDITOR: Maryanne Blacker
FOOD EDITOR: Pamela Clark

• • •

DESIGNERS: Paula Wooller, Robbylee Phelan

• • •

DEPUTY FOOD EDITOR: Jan Castorina
ASSISTANT FOOD EDITOR: Kathy Snowball
ASSOCIATE FOOD EDITOR: Enid Morrison
SENIOR HOME ECONOMISTS: Alexandra McCowan, Louise Patniotis, Kathy Wharton
HOME ECONOMISTS: Cynthia Black, Leisel Chen, Tracey Port, Kathy McGarry, Maggie Quickenden, Dimitra Stais
EDITORIAL CO-ORDINATOR: Elizabeth Hooper
KITCHEN ASSISTANT: Amy Wong

• • •

STYLISTS: Lucy Andrews, Marie-Helene Clauzon, Rosemary de Santis, Carolyn Fienberg, Jane Hann, Jacqui Hing
PHOTOGRAPHERS: Kevin Brown, Robert Clark, Robert Taylor, Jon Waddy

• • •

HOME LIBRARY STAFF:

ASSISTANT EDITOR: Beverley Hudec
EDITORIAL COORDINATOR: Lara Quinlin

• • •

ACP PUBLISHER: Richard Walsh
ACP ASSOCIATE PUBLISHER: Bob Neil

• • •

Produced by The Australian Women's Weekly Home Library. Typeset by Photoset Computer Service Pty Ltd, and Letter Perfect, Sydney. Printed by Dai Nippon Co., Ltd in Japan. Published by Australian Consolidated Press, 54 Park Street Sydney.
♦ **AUSTRALIA:** Distributed by Network Distribution Company, 54 Park Street Sydney, (02) 282 8777.
♦ **UNITED KINGDOM:** Distributed in the U.K. by Australian Consolidated Press (UK) Ltd, 20 Galowhill Rd, Brackmills, Northampton NN4 OEE (0604) 760 456.
♦ **CANADA:** Distributed in Canada by Whitecap Books Ltd, 1086 West 3rd St, North Vancouver V7P 3J6 (604) 980 9852.
♦ **NEW ZEALAND:** Distributed in New Zealand by Netlink Distribution Company, 17B Hargreaves St, Level 5, College Hill, Auckland 1 (9) 302 7616.
♦ **SOUTH AFRICA:** Distributed in South Africa by Intermag, PO Box 57394, Springfield 2137 (011) 493 3200. ACN 000 031 747.

• • •

Dinner Party Cookbook No. 3

Includes index.
ISBN 0 949128 91 0.

1. Diners and dining. 2. Menus.
3. Cookery (Series : Australian Women's Weekly Home Library).

641.568

• • •

© A C P 1992
This publication is copyright. No part of it may be reproduced or transmitted in any form without the written permission of the publishers.

• • •

COVER: Veal Medallions with Mustard and Prosciutto, page 15, Creamy Kumara Puree and Watercress Pepper Salad, page 17.
OPPOSITE: Marinated Scallops with Pancetta and Olives, page 37.
BACK COVER: Rich Chocolate Meringue and Mousse Cake, page 26.

B/C 040126

With our fresh, fun and innovative dinner parties, you'll have terrific ideas for entertaining whatever the occasion. Menus show instantly what you'll eat, with wine styles selected by Australian wine writer Alan Hill. However, wines can be omitted, if you prefer. We suggest you do as much planning and advance preparation as possible so you're free to relax and spend time with your guests; you'll find helpful tips in our recipes, and more on page 125.

Pamela Clark
FOOD EDITOR

BRITISH & NORTH AMERICAN READERS: Please note that Australian cup and spoon measurements are metric. Conversion charts for cup and spoon measurements and oven temperatures appear on page 125. A glossary explaining unfamiliar terms and ingredients appears on page 122.

Tasty New Classics

Serves 6

Goats' Cheese and Asparagus Terrine
dry semillon or chablis

❦

Buttered Spatchcocks with Redcurrant Glaze
Wild Rice and Risoni
Stir-Fried Vegetable Sticks
dry semillon or chablis
or a medium-bodied pinot noir

❦

Crepes with Orange Creme Patissiere
botrytis semillon sweet white

❦

We've given delicious new twists to some classics in this very stylish
menu. First, there's the tang of goats' cheese in a leek-wrapped
terrine. Then we've made a redcurrant wine glaze for the
spatchcocks, with crunchy vegetables and wild rice and pasta for
taste and texture contrast. To follow, dessert crepes conceal a zesty
orange cream. The terrine can be made 2 days ahead, but the main
course is cooked and served immediately. The dessert is quick to
assemble just before serving.

GOATS' CHEESE AND ASPARAGUS TERRINE

3/4 bunch (about 185g) fresh
   asparagus spears
1 medium (about 350g) leek
50g butter
12 green shallots, chopped
150g packaged cream cheese
300g goats' cheese
2 teaspoons gelatine
1 tablespoon water
300ml carton thickened cream

TOMATO VINAIGRETTE
1 small (about 170g) green
   cucumber, seeded
1 large (about 300g) tomato, seeded
2 tablespoons white vinegar
1/4 cup olive oil
1/4 teaspoon French mustard
1/4 teaspoon sugar

Lightly oil loaf dish (6 cup capacity). Line with plastic wrap. Boil, steam or microwave asparagus until just tender, drain, rinse under cold water.

Cut leek in half lengthways. Add leaves to pan of boiling water, boil 30 seconds, drain, rinse under cold water, pat dry with absorbent paper. Using sharp knife, scrape inside surface of leaves to remove membrane. Line base and sides of prepared dish with leek leaves, allowing ends to overhang sides of dish.

Heat butter in pan, add shallots, cook, stirring, until soft; cool. Beat cheeses and shallot mixture in large bowl with electric mixer until combined. Sprinkle gelatine over water in cup, stand in small pan of simmering water, stir until dissolved; cool 10 minutes. Add gelatine mixture and cream to cheese mixture, beat until mixture is just combined.

Pour filling into prepared dish, place asparagus over cheese mixture, fold leek leaves over to cover filling. Cover, refrigerate several hours or overnight.

Just before serving, slice terrine, serve with tomato vinaigrette.

Tomato Vinaigrette: Chop cucumber and tomato finely. Combine all ingredients in bowl; mix well.

- Terrine can be made 2 days ahead; tomato vinaigrette best made just before serving.
- Storage: Covered, in refrigerator.
- Freeze: Not suitable.
- Microwave: Asparagus, leek and shallot mixture suitable.

BUTTERED SPATCHCOCKS WITH REDCURRANT GLAZE

6 x size 5 spatchcocks
125g butter
1 clove garlic, crushed
1 teaspoon cumin seeds
1/2 teaspoon paprika
1 tablespoon honey

REDCURRANT GLAZE
3/4 cup dry red wine
1/2 cup redcurrant jelly
3 teaspoons white vinegar
1 tablespoon cornflour
3/4 cup water

Place spatchcocks on wire rack in baking dish. Melt butter in pan, stir in garlic, seeds, paprika and honey. Brush inside and outside of spatchcocks with butter mixture. Bake, uncovered, in moderate oven about 45 minutes or until cooked through. Serve buttered spatchcocks with redcurrant glaze.

Redcurrant Glaze: Combine wine, jelly and vinegar in pan, stir over heat until smooth. Stir in blended cornflour and water, stir over heat until glaze boils and thickens slightly.

- Recipe best made just before serving.
- Freeze: Not suitable.
- Microwave: Not suitable.

WILD RICE AND RISONI

1 cup (170g) wild rice
½ cup risoni pasta
20g butter
1 medium (about 150g) onion,
**   chopped**
1 clove garlic, crushed
2 tablespoons honey
1 teaspoon light soy sauce
1 teaspoon lemon juice
2 tablespoons chopped fresh parsley

Bring large pan of water to boil, add rice, boil, uncovered, 25 minutes; drain. Bring another large pan of water to boil, add risoni, boil, uncovered, about 10 minutes or until risoni is tender; drain.

Heat butter in pan, add onion and garlic, cook, stirring, until onion is soft. Add rice, risoni, honey, sauce, juice and parsley, stir until heated through.

- Wild rice and risoni can be cooked a day ahead.
- Freeze: Not suitable.
- Microwave: Suitable.

STIR-FRIED VEGETABLE STICKS

3 medium (about 360g) carrots
1 large (150g) zucchini
6 green shallots
200g snow peas
2 tablespoons oil
2 cloves garlic, crushed

Cut carrots, zucchini and shallots into thin strips. Halve snow peas lengthways.

Just before serving, heat oil in wok or pan, add carrots, zucchini and garlic, stir-fry 3 minutes. Add remaining ingredients, stir-fry until vegetables are just tender.

- Recipe best made just before serving.
- Freeze: Not suitable.
- Microwave: Not suitable.

LEFT: Goats' Cheese and Asparagus Terrine.
ABOVE: Buttered Spatchcocks with Redcurrant Glaze, Wild Rice and Risoni, and Stir-Fried Vegetable Sticks.

China and glassware from Royal Doulton; cutlery and salt and pepper set from The Bay Tree; table linen from Accoutrement.

CREPES WITH ORANGE CREME PATISSIERE

2 medium (about 400g) oranges
1 cup plain flour
2 teaspoons castor sugar
4 eggs
2 tablespoons oil
1½ cups milk

ORANGE CREME PATISSIERE
1¼ cups milk
2 teaspoons grated orange rind
1 egg
2 egg yolks
1 tablespoon plain flour
1 tablespoon cornflour
¼ cup castor sugar
1 tablespoon Grand Marnier

ORANGE GLAZE
¼ cup lime juice
1 cup orange juice
⅓ cup honey
1½ teaspoons cornflour
1½ teaspoons water
¼ cup Grand Marnier

CARAMELISED PEEL
1 medium orange
1 medium lemon
2 medium limes
½ cup castor sugar
¼ cup water

Peel oranges, cut between membranes into segments, remove any remaining pith and seeds; reserve any juice for glaze.

Sift flour and sugar into bowl, gradually stir in combined eggs, oil and milk; beat until smooth. Cover, stand 30 minutes. Pour 2 tablespoons of batter into heated greased heavy-based pan; cook until lightly browned underneath. Turn crepe, brown other side. Repeat with remaining batter. You will need 18 crepes for this recipe. Cut crepes into 10cm rounds.

Just before serving, top half of each crepe with 2 teaspoons of orange creme patissiere, fold over to enclose filling. Serve crepes with orange segments, orange glaze and caramelised peel.

Orange Creme Patissiere: Heat 1 cup of the milk and rind in pan until almost boiling. Beat remaining milk, egg, egg yolks, flour, cornflour and sugar in small bowl with electric mixer until smooth, gradually beat in hot milk mixture while motor is operating. Return to pan, stir over heat until mixture boils and thickens. Remove from heat, stir in liqueur, cover; cool.

Orange Glaze: Using any reserved juice, combine juices and honey in pan, bring to boil, stir in blended cornflour and water, stir over heat until mixture boils and thickens slightly; stir in liqueur, strain.

Caramelised Peel: Remove peel thinly from orange, lemon and limes using a vegetable peeler; cut peel into fine strips. Combine sugar and water in pan, stir over heat, without boiling, until sugar is dissolved. Boil, uncovered, without stirring, until syrup is golden brown. Remove pan from heat, stir in peel; strain, discard syrup. Cool peel on lightly oiled tray.

■ Unfilled crepes and orange creme patissiere can be made a day ahead. Orange glaze and caramelised peel can be made 3 hours ahead.
■ Storage: Covered, in refrigerator.
■ Freeze: Unfilled crepes suitable.
■ Microwave: Not suitable.

ABOVE: Crepes with Orange Creme Patissiere.

Quick and Easy

Serves 6

Pasta with Creamy Sun-Dried Tomato Sauce

buttery chardonnay or chilled medium dry sherry

❧

Sake Marinated Quail

Eggplant Crisps

Leafy Salad with Lime Vinaigrette

pinot noir

❧

Glazed Peaches with Honey Yogurt

late-picked spatlese-style riesling

❧

Just buy a few special ingredients on the way home, and you're off to a flying start with these easy recipes. Everything can be made with minimum time and fuss.

For example, the entree is pasta with freshly made sauce. To follow, marinated quail are deep-fried and served with pre-cooked eggplant crisps and a quick salad. Then it's under the griller for poached peaches with their prepared marzipan filling; the honey yogurt is almost instant, but can also be made ahead.

PASTA WITH CREAMY SUN-DRIED TOMATO SAUCE

2 medium (about 400g) red peppers
2 tablespoons olive oil
2 medium (about 300g) onions, sliced
2 cloves garlic, crushed
6 green shallots, chopped
½ teaspoon chopped fresh chilli
½ cup drained sun-dried tomatoes, thinly sliced
½ cup dry white wine
300ml carton cream
⅓ cup sour cream
⅓ cup shredded fresh basil
1 cup (80g) grated parmesan cheese
300g spaghettini pasta
20g parmesan cheese, extra
2 tablespoons shredded fresh basil, extra

Quarter peppers, remove seeds and membranes. Grill peppers, skin side up, until skin blisters and blackens. Cool peppers, peel away and discard skin, cut peppers into thin strips.

Heat oil in pan, add onions and garlic, cook, stirring, until onions are soft. Add peppers, shallots, chilli and tomatoes, cook, stirring, until shallots are soft. Stir in wine, creams, basil and grated cheese, stir until heated through; do not boil.

Meanwhile, add pasta to large pan of boiling water, boil, uncovered, until pasta is just tender; drain, stir sauce into pasta.

Using vegetable peeler, shave flakes from extra parmesan cheese. Serve pasta sprinkled with flaked extra cheese and extra basil.

- Recipe best made just before serving.
- Freeze: Not suitable.
- Microwave: Pasta suitable.

SAKE MARINATED QUAIL

12 quail
¾ cup sake
2 tablespoons mirin
⅓ cup light soy sauce
½ cup brown sugar
⅔ cup sweet sherry
2 tablespoons grated fresh ginger
4 cloves garlic, crushed
3 green shallots, chopped
oil for deep-frying
1 tablespoon cornflour
½ cup chicken stock

Tie quail legs with string; tuck wings under bodies. Bring large pan of water to the boil, add quail to water in batches, simmer 2 minutes; drain quail, discard water.

Combine sake, mirin, soy sauce, sugar, sherry, ginger, garlic and shallots in large bowl. Add quail, cover, refrigerate several hours or overnight; turn quail occasionally.

Drain quail; reserve marinade. Deep-fry quail in hot oil in batches until browned and tender, drain on absorbent paper; keep warm.

Place reserved marinade in pan, simmer until reduced by one-third, stir in blended cornflour and stock, stir over heat until sauce boils and thickens. Serve quail with sauce. Serve with eggplant crisps and leafy salad with lime vinaigrette.

- Recipe can be prepared a day ahead.
- Storage: Covered, in refrigerator.
- Freeze: Not suitable.
- Microwave: Sauce suitable.

EGGPLANT CRISPS

2 medium (about 650g) eggplants
coarse cooking salt
oil for shallow-frying

Cut eggplants into very thin slices. Sprinkle eggplants with salt, stand 15 minutes. Rinse eggplants under cold water, drain, pat dry with absorbent paper.

Heat oil in pan, cook eggplants over low heat in batches until browned and crisp; drain on absorbent paper. Crisps can be served warm or cold.

- Recipe can be made 2 days ahead.
- Storage: Airtight container.
- Freeze: Not suitable.
- Microwave: Not suitable.

LEFT: Pasta with Creamy Sun-Dried Tomato Sauce.
ABOVE: Eggplant Crisps.
RIGHT: Sake Marinated Quail with Eggplant Crisps.

LEAFY SALAD WITH LIME VINAIGRETTE

2 small (about 340g) green cucumbers
200g snow peas
1 mignonette lettuce
1 radicchio lettuce
1 small bunch watercress sprigs
2 medium (about 500g) avocados

LIME VINAIGRETTE
2 tablespoons macadamia nut oil
¼ cup lime juice
2 tablespoons chopped fresh chives
1 tablespoon chopped fresh thyme
1 tablespoon shredded fresh basil

Using vegetable peeler, peel cucumbers lengthways to form long strips. Place snow peas in pan of boiling water, return to the boil, drain; rinse under cold water, drain. Combine cucumbers, snow peas, torn lettuce and watercress in large bowl.

Just before serving, slice avocados, add to salad mixture. Toss salad lightly with lime vinaigrette.

Lime Vinaigrette: Combine all ingredients in jar; shake well.

■ Lime vinaigrette can be made several hours ahead.
■ Storage: Covered, in refrigerator.
■ Freeze: Not suitable.
■ Microwave: Snow peas suitable.

ABOVE: Leafy Salad with Lime Vinaigrette.
RIGHT: Glazed Peaches with Honey Yogurt.

China, glassware, jug, sugar bowl, and cutlery from The Bay Tree Kitchen Shop; serviettes from Between the Sheets; salad servers from Hale Imports.

GLAZED PEACHES WITH HONEY YOGURT

2 cups water
1 cup sugar
6 medium (about 1.2kg) slipstone peaches, halved

CHEESE FILLING
125g packet cream cheese, softened
100g prepared marzipan
½ teaspoon ground nutmeg

HONEY YOGURT
200g carton plain yogurt
1 tablespoon honey

Combine water and sugar in pan, stir over heat, without boiling, until sugar is dissolved. Bring sugar syrup to boil, reduce heat, add peach halves, simmer, covered, 4 minutes. Remove peaches carefully; discard sugar syrup. Cool peaches 10 minutes; remove skin from peaches.

Just before serving, press cheese filling into peach centres, grill until filling is soft. Serve with honey yogurt.

Cheese Filling: Beat all ingredients in small bowl with electric mixer until just combined. Roll mixture into 12 balls.

Honey Yogurt: Combine all ingredients in bowl; mix well.

■ Cheese filling and honey yogurt can be made a day ahead.
■ Storage: Covered, in refrigerator.
■ Freeze: Not suitable.
■ Microwave: Not suitable.

Dining with the Boss

Serves 6

Marinated Olives with Rosemary and Thyme

sparkling white wine

Smoked Salmon Pastries with Chive Butter Sauce

sparkling white wine

Veal Medallions with Mustard and Prosciutto

Creamy Kumara Puree

Watercress Pepper Salad

pinot noir

Chocolate Orange Meringue Gateau

sauternes-style white wine

Fresh, interesting and uncomplicated, this menu will certainly impress the boss. Lots can be done ahead, such as marinating the olives, baking the pastry cases, preparing the veal, salad and gateau layers. The pastries have more baking just before serving, and the veal is cooked then, too; each has an easy sauce. You'll need about 50 minutes to bake the kumara. Meanwhile, assemble the gateau layers about 2 hours before serving.

MARINATED OLIVES WITH ROSEMARY AND THYME

200g green olives, drained
200g black olives, drained
1½ cups olive oil
½ cup lemon juice
2 tablespoons fresh thyme leaves
⅓ cup fresh rosemary leaves
2 cloves garlic, sliced

Combine all ingredients in jar. Shake jar occasionally.

■ Olives must be marinated at least 10 days ahead.
■ Storage: In cool, dark cupboard.
■ Freeze: Not suitable.

SMOKED SALMON PASTRIES WITH CHIVE BUTTER SAUCE

3 sheets ready-rolled puff pastry
1 egg yolk
18 slices (about 450g) smoked salmon
2 medium (about 260g) tomatoes, seeded, chopped

CHIVE BUTTER SAUCE
2 tablespoons dry white wine
2 tablespoons white vinegar
180g butter, chopped
1 tablespoon chopped fresh chives

Make base pattern by cutting 8cm x 12cm rectangle from paper. Make frame by cutting another 8cm x 12cm rectangle from paper; inside this, cut a 6cm x 10cm rectangle, leaving 1cm frame.

Using base pattern, cut 6 rectangles from 1 sheet of pastry. Place rectangles onto ungreased oven trays.

Brush 1 sheet of remaining pastry with water, top with remaining sheet of pastry; press to seal. Using frame pattern, cut 6 frame shapes from layered pastry; discard pastry scraps. Brush edges of bases with water, press frames onto bases, forming shallow pastry cases. Cover, refrigerate several hours or overnight.

Brush tops of frames with egg yolk, bake in very hot oven about 6 minutes or

until pastry is browned and risen.

Place 3 slices of salmon into each pastry case, bake, covered, in moderately hot oven about 15 minutes or until heated through. Place cases on serving plates, spoon over about 2 teaspoons of chive butter sauce. Drizzle remaining sauce around cases, sprinkle with tomatoes.

Chive Butter Sauce: Combine wine and vinegar in pan, simmer, uncovered, until reduced to 1 tablespoon. Gradually whisk in cold butter over low heat. Stir in chives.

■ Pastries should be assembled just before serving. Cases can be made 2 days ahead. Chive butter sauce best made just before serving.
■ Storage: Cases, in airtight container.
■ Freeze: Cases suitable.
■ Microwave: Not suitable.

LEFT: Marinated Olives with Rosemary and Thyme.
ABOVE: Smoked Salmon Pastries with Chive Butter Sauce.
RIGHT: Veal Medallions with Mustard and Prosciutto, and Creamy Kumara Puree.

VEAL MEDALLIONS WITH MUSTARD AND PROSCIUTTO

8 spinach (silverbeet) leaves, approximately
1 tablespoon Dijon mustard
1 tablespoon French mustard
1 tablespoon seeded mustard
2 teaspoons grated lemon rind
1 tablespoon chopped fresh dill
4 x 300g veal fillets
40 slices (about 400g) prosciutto
1½ tablespoons oil
3 cloves garlic, crushed
¾ cup dry sherry
1½ tablespoons Dijon mustard, extra
2 cups beef stock
2 teaspoons cornflour
1½ tablespoons water
2 tablespoons chopped fresh dill, extra

Boil, steam or microwave spinach until just wilted, rinse in cold water; drain, pat dry. Place quarter of the spinach slightly overlapping to form a rectangle the same length as a piece of veal. Spread quarter of the combined mustards, rind, and dill onto a piece of veal, place veal onto spinach, roll up like a Swiss roll.

Place quarter of the prosciutto on board, slightly overlapping in 2 rows to form a rectangle. Place rolled veal onto prosciutto, roll up like a Swiss roll. Repeat process with remaining veal, mustard mixture, spinach and prosciutto.

Heat oil in baking dish, add rolls, cook, turning occasionally, until prosciutto is lightly browned. Bake, uncovered, in very hot oven about 15 minutes or until veal is cooked as desired. Remove rolls from baking dish; keep warm.

Place baking dish over heat, add garlic and sherry, boil 2 minutes. Add extra mustard, stock and blended cornflour and water; stir over heat until sauce boils and thickens. Strain sauce, stir in extra dill.

Slice veal thickly, serve with sauce. Serve with creamy kumara puree and watercress pepper salad.

■ Recipe can be prepared a day ahead.
■ Storage: Covered, in refrigerator.
■ Freeze: Not suitable.
■ Microwave: Spinach suitable.

CREAMY KUMARA PUREE

1 large (about 550g) kumara
⅔ cup thickened cream
¼ teaspoon ground cumin
¼ teaspoon mixed spice

Cut kumara into 4cm chunks, place onto oven tray, cover, bake in moderately hot oven about 50 minutes or until tender.

Process kumara with remaining ingredients until smooth.

- ■ Recipe best made just before serving.
- ■ Freeze: Not suitable.
- ■ Microwave: Suitable.

LEFT: Veal Medallions with Mustard and Prosciutto, Creamy Kumara Puree and Watercress Pepper Salad.
BELOW: Chocolate Orange Meringue Gateau.

China and glassware from Waterford Wedgwood; cutlery from Noritake.

WATERCRESS PEPPER SALAD

2 cups (about 120g) firmly packed watercress sprigs
6 green shallots, chopped
1 medium (about 200g) green pepper, sliced
1 medium (about 200g) red pepper, sliced
1 medium (about 200g) yellow pepper, sliced

DRESSING
¼ cup lime juice
1 teaspoon honey
1 tablespoon olive oil
1 teaspoon seasoned pepper

Combine watercress, shallots and peppers in bowl. Drizzle dressing over salad.
Dressing: Combine all ingredients in jar; shake well.

- ■ Salad best made just before serving.
- ■ Freeze: Not suitable.

CHOCOLATE ORANGE MERINGUE GATEAU

It is correct that this cake contains no flour.

100g dark chocolate, melted
100g unsalted butter, melted
1 tablespoon Grand Marnier
2 tablespoons water
⅔ cup castor sugar
⅔ cup packaged ground almonds
3 eggs, separated

ORANGE CREAM
6 egg yolks
2 teaspoons grated orange rind
½ cup castor sugar
½ cup orange juice
2 teaspoons gelatine
1 tablespoon water
⅔ cup thickened cream

MERINGUE
3 egg whites
¾ cup castor sugar
3 teaspoons cornflour
1 teaspoon lemon juice

Grease deep 20cm round cake pan, cover base with paper, grease paper. Combine chocolate, butter, liqueur, water, sugar and nuts in large bowl; stir in egg yolks. Beat egg whites in small bowl until soft peaks form, fold into chocolate mixture, pour mixture into prepared pan. Bake in moderate oven about 45 minutes or until cake is firm; cool in pan.

Carefully turn cake from pan, place cake onto serving plate. Spread top with orange cream, top with meringue layer; refrigerate 2 hours before serving.
Orange Cream: Beat egg yolks, rind and sugar in small bowl with electric mixer until thick and creamy. Gradually beat in juice. Transfer mixture to pan, stir over low heat, without boiling, for about 20 minutes or until mixture thickens. Remove from heat. Sprinkle gelatine over water in cup, stand in small pan of simmering water, stir until gelatine is dissolved, stir into warm orange mixture. Beat cream until soft peaks form, then fold cream into orange mixture; cool.
Meringue: Cover oven tray with foil, grease foil, dust with a little plain flour, shake away excess flour. Mark a 17cm diameter circle on foil. Beat egg whites, sugar, cornflour and juice in small bowl with electric mixer for about 10 minutes or until sugar is dissolved. Spread mixture over circle. Bake in very slow oven for about 1½ hours or until meringue is dry and firm to touch. Cool meringue in oven with door ajar.

- ■ Cake and meringue can be made a day ahead. Assemble gateau 2 hours before serving.
- ■ Storage: Cake and meringue, separately, in airtight containers.
- ■ Freeze: Not suitable.
- ■ Microwave: Not suitable.

Style without Expense

Serves 8

Zucchini and Feta Spiral with Tomato Sauce
dry sparkling wine

❧

Spicy Meatballs with Garlic Yogurt Sauce
Crispy Onion Rings
Saffron Rice
spicy shiraz or Italian-style red

❧

Creamy Chocolate and Caramel Mousse
dry sparkling wine

❧

Our colourful, imaginative recipes give you an easy, top-value dinner for 8 while spending lots less. All except the onions can be cooked ahead and reheated. The delicious fillo pastry spiral can be made 2 days ahead. Spicy meatballs, of course, are quick to put together a day ahead; do the garlic yogurt sauce, saffron rice and creamy cold mousse about the same time. That leaves only the crispy onion rings to deep-fry just before serving.

ZUCCHINI AND FETA SPIRAL WITH TOMATO SAUCE

2 tablespoons olive oil
1 medium (about 170g) red Spanish
    onion, sliced
1 teaspoon caraway seeds, crushed
5 medium (about 500g) zucchini,
    coarsely grated
400g feta cheese, finely chopped
1 egg, lightly beaten
14 sheets fillo pastry
125g butter, melted
1 egg, lightly beaten, extra
1 tablespoon grated parmesan
    cheese
½ teaspoon caraway seeds, extra

TOMATO SAUCE
1 tablespoon oil
1 medium (about 150g) onion, sliced
2 cloves garlic, sliced
2 bay leaves
2 x 400g cans tomatoes
1 tablespoon tomato paste
1 teaspoon sugar
½ cup water

Grease 30cm pizza pan. Heat oil in medium pan, add onion and seeds, cook, stirring, until onion is soft. Add zucchini, stir over heat until zucchini is soft and most of the liquid has evaporated. Remove from heat, stir in feta cheese; cool, stir in egg.

Layer 2 pastry sheets together, brushing each with butter. Spread ½ cup zucchini mixture loosely down 1 long edge of pastry, leaving 3cm border at each end. Roll pastry lightly around mixture, tucking in ends while rolling. Repeat with remaining pastry, butter and zucchini mixture.

Coil pastry rolls on pizza pan, starting from centre and working out to edge of pan to form a spiral, brushing sides of roll with extra egg as you work. Sprinkle spiral with combined parmesan cheese and extra seeds. Bake in moderate oven about 20 minutes or until browned. Serve with tomato sauce.

Tomato Sauce: Heat oil in pan, add onion, garlic and bay leaves, cook, stirring, until onion is soft. Add undrained crushed tomatoes, paste, sugar and water. Simmer 15 minutes, discard bay leaves. Blend or process half mixture until smooth, return to remaining mixture in pan. Reheat before serving.

■ Recipe can be made 2 days ahead.
■ Storage: Covered, in refrigerator.
■ Freeze: Suitable.
■ Microwave: Tomato sauce suitable.

SPICY MEATBALLS WITH GARLIC YOGURT SAUCE

4 medium (about 800g) green peppers
4 medium (about 800g) red peppers
1 tablespoon oil
1 large (about 200g) onion, chopped
2 cloves garlic, crushed
1 teaspoon ground cumin
1 teaspoon ground coriander
2 teaspoons curry powder
1 teaspoon sambal oelek
1kg minced beef
1 egg, lightly beaten
1 cup (70g) stale breadcrumbs
oil for deep-frying

GARLIC YOGURT SAUCE

500g carton plain yogurt
1 clove garlic, crushed
½ teaspoon sambal oelek
2 tablespoons chopped fresh
coriander

Quarter peppers, remove seeds and membranes. Grill peppers, skin side up, until skin blisters and blackens. Peel away skin, cut peppers into wide strips.

Heat oil in pan, add onion, garlic and spices, cook, stirring, until onion is soft; cool. Combine onion mixture in bowl with mince, egg and breadcrumbs. Roll level tablespoons of mixture into balls. Deep-fry meatballs in hot oil until browned and cooked through. Serve meatballs over peppers, topped with garlic yogurt sauce.

Garlic Yogurt Sauce: Combine all ingredients in pan, stir over heat until heated through.

- Recipe can be made a day ahead.
- Storage: Covered, in refrigerator.
- Freeze: Meatballs suitable.
- Microwave: Garlic yogurt sauce suitable.

CRISPY ONION RINGS

2 large (about 800g) onions
plain flour
2 eggs, lightly beaten
1 cup (80g) grated parmesan cheese
2 cups (140g) stale breadcrumbs
2 teaspoons seasoned pepper
oil for deep-frying

Cut onions into 5mm slices. Toss rings in flour; dip into eggs, then combined cheese, breadcrumbs and pepper. Refrigerate onion rings 1 hour. Deep-fry onion rings in hot oil until browned and crisp; drain on absorbent paper.

- Onion rings can be prepared a day ahead.
- Storage: Covered, in refrigerator.
- Freeze: Not suitable.
- Microwave: Not suitable.

SAFFRON RICE

3 cups white rice
pinch saffron powder

Add rice to large pan of boiling water, stir in saffron, simmer, uncovered, until rice is just tender; drain.

- Rice can be cooked a day ahead.
- Storage: Covered, in refrigerator.
- Freeze: Suitable.
- Microwave: Suitable.

LEFT: Zucchini and Feta Spiral with Tomato Sauce.
RIGHT: Spicy Meatballs with Garlic Yogurt Sauce, Crispy Onion Rings and Saffron Rice.

CREAMY CHOCOLATE AND CARAMEL MOUSSE

1 cup thickened cream
200g dark chocolate, melted
2 egg whites
1 tablespoon castor sugar
¼ cup slivered almonds, toasted

CARAMEL MOUSSE
250g Jersey caramels
1 tablespoon milk
2 eggs, separated
2 teaspoons gelatine
1 tablespoon water
1 cup thickened cream
1 tablespoon castor sugar

Beat cream in medium bowl until soft peaks form. Lightly fold cooled chocolate into cream. Beat egg whites in small bowl until soft peaks form, add sugar, beat until dissolved. Lightly fold egg white mixture into chocolate mixture in 2 batches.

Divide the mousse between 8 glasses (¾ cup capacity), top with caramel mousse, smooth surface of mousses, refrigerate several hours or overnight. Serve sprinkled with nuts.

Caramel Mousse: Combine caramels and milk in pan, stir over low heat, without boiling, until caramels are melted. Transfer to large bowl, stir in egg yolks. Sprinkle gelatine over water in cup, stand in small pan of simmering water, stir until dissolved. Stir into caramel mixture; cool until almost set. Beat cream in small bowl until soft peaks form. Fold cream into caramel mixture. Beat egg whites in small bowl until soft peaks form, add sugar, beat until dissolved. Gently fold egg white mixture into caramel mixture in 2 batches.

■ Recipe can be made a day ahead.
■ Storage: Covered, in refrigerator.
■ Freeze: Not suitable.
■ Microwave: Gelatine mixture and chocolate suitable.

BELOW: Creamy Chocolate and Caramel Mousse.

China from Wedgwood; cutlery from The Culinary Delight; tablecloth and serviettes from Lillywhites.

Light Race Day Lunch

Serves 10

Sparkling Strawberry Cocktails
Savoury Puffs with Two Fillings

**Cold Fillet of Veal with
Tuna Mayonnaise**
Potato Salad with Herbed Vinaigrette
full-flavoured chardonnay

**Rich Chocolate Meringue and
Mousse Cake**
sparkling red burgundy

The champagne mood of a big race day is matched by our light and pretty lunch. It's all
cold, starting with freshly mixed strawberry cocktails and savoury puffs
assembled just before serving. For the main course, delicate veal is accompanied by tuna
mayonnaise and herbed potato salad, all done ahead. Then comes a show-off chocolate
meringue and mousse cake layered the day before and decorated just before serving.

SAVOURY PUFFS WITH TWO FILLINGS

1 cup water
80g butter, chopped
1 cup plain flour
1 teaspoon garlic salt
4 eggs

TWO FILLINGS
60g butter
¼ cup plain flour
1¼ cups milk
2 tablespoons grated parmesan cheese
½ cup sour cream
2 tablespoons cream
1 tablespoon oil
1 small (about 80g) onion, chopped
2 tablespoons drained chopped sun-dried tomatoes
1 (about 220g) smoked trout
2 teaspoons chopped fresh thyme
1 tablespoon chopped fresh chives
2 teaspoons chopped fresh dill

Combine water and butter in pan, bring to boil, stirring, until butter is melted. Add sifted flour and garlic salt all at once, stir vigorously over heat until mixture leaves side of pan and forms a smooth ball.

Transfer mixture to small bowl of electric mixer or processor. Add eggs 1 at a time while motor is operating, beat until smooth after each addition. Drop ½ level tablespoons of mixture about 3cm apart onto lightly greased oven trays. Bake in hot oven about 10 minutes, reduce heat, bake further 15 minutes or until puffs are browned and crisp.

Make a small slit in side of puffs to allow steam to escape, return to moderate oven on trays for about 10 minutes or until dry. Cool on wire rack. Cut each puff in half.

Just before serving, spoon onion and tomato mixture into half the puff bases and trout mixture into remaining puff bases. Replace tops.

Two Fillings: Melt butter in pan, add flour, cook, stirring, until mixture is dry and grainy. Remove from heat, gradually stir in milk, stir over heat until mixture boils and thickens. Remove from heat, stir in cheese, cool 5 minutes. Stir in both creams. Divide mixture into 2 bowls.

Heat oil in pan, add onion, cook, stirring, until soft. Stir onion mixture and tomatoes into 1 bowl. Remove and discard skin and bones from trout; flake trout. Stir trout and herbs into remaining bowl of cheese mixture.

Makes about 40.

- Puffs and fillings can be prepared a day ahead.
- Storage: Puffs, in airtight container. Fillings, covered, in refrigerator.
- Freeze: Unfilled puffs suitable.
- Microwave: Not suitable.

ABOVE: Sparkling Strawberry Cocktails, Savoury Puffs with Two Fillings.
RIGHT: Cold Fillet of Veal with Tuna Mayonnaise and Potato Salad with Herbed Vinaigrette.

China and glassware from Waterford Wedgwood; napery, curtain, gold box and tassel from Between the Sheets; cutlery from David Jones.

SPARKLING STRAWBERRY COCKTAILS

750g strawberries
¼ cup icing sugar
1 litre (4 cups) lemonade
750ml bottle dry sparkling wine

Blend or process strawberries and sugar until smooth. Combine strawberry mixture, lemonade and wine in large jug.

- Recipe best made just before serving.

COLD FILLET OF VEAL WITH TUNA MAYONNAISE

4 medium (about 1.4kg) leeks
3 cups chicken stock
5 medium (about 1kg) red peppers
30g butter
2 tablespoons oil
1.5kg veal fillet
¼ cup drained capers

TUNA MAYONNAISE
3 egg yolks
1½ tablespoons lemon juice
½ cup olive oil
½ cup oil
2 cloves garlic, crushed
2 tablespoons drained capers, chopped
425g can tuna in brine, drained
⅔ cup thickened cream

Cut leeks in half lengthways, separate leaves. Heat stock in pan, simmer, uncovered, 2 minutes. Add leeks, cook in batches for 30 seconds, drain on absorbent paper. Quarter peppers, remove seeds and membranes, grill peppers, skin side up, until skin blisters and blackens, peel away and discard skin. Cut peppers into 2cm strips.

Heat butter and oil in pan, add veal, cook until browned all over. Transfer veal to wire rack in baking dish. Bake, uncovered, in moderately hot oven about 20 minutes or until cooked as desired; cool.

Just before serving, slice veal, serve with leeks, red peppers, tuna mayonnaise and capers.

Tuna Mayonnaise: Blend or process egg yolks and juice until smooth. Add oils gradually while motor is operating; blend until thick. Add garlic, capers, tuna and cream, blend until smooth.

- Recipe can be made a day ahead.
- Storage: Covered, in refrigerator.
- Freeze: Not suitable.
- Microwave: Not suitable.

POTATO SALAD WITH HERBED VINAIGRETTE

2kg baby new potatoes, halved

HERBED VINAIGRETTE
2 tablespoons tarragon vinegar
¼ cup red wine vinegar
⅓ cup olive oil
2 teaspoons French mustard
2 teaspoons paprika
2 teaspoons chopped fresh basil
2 tablespoons chopped fresh chives
2 tablespoons chopped fresh parsley
2 tablespoons chopped fresh thyme

Boil, steam or microwave potatoes until tender, drain. Combine potatoes and herbed vinaigrette in bowl, cool, cover, refrigerate.

Herbed Vinaigrette: Combine all ingredients in jar; shake well.

- Recipe can be made a day ahead.
- Storage: Covered, in refrigerator.
- Freeze: Not suitable.
- Microwave: Potatoes suitable.

RICH CHOCOLATE MERINGUE AND MOUSSE CAKE

8 egg whites
2 cups castor sugar
1/3 cup cocoa

MOUSSE FILLING
1/2 cup packaged ground hazelnuts
2 teaspoons gelatine
1 tablespoon water
300g dark chocolate, melted
8 egg yolks
2 tablespoons brandy
600ml carton thickened cream

CHOCOLATE LACE
100g Choc Melts, melted

Cover 4 oven trays with baking paper, mark 23cm circles on paper on 3 of the trays. Beat 4 of the egg whites in large bowl with electric mixer until soft peaks form. Gradually add 1 cup of the sugar, beat until dissolved between additions. Fold in 2 tablespoons of the sifted cocoa.

Spoon mixture into piping bag fitted with 2cm tube. Pipe meringue inside 2 of the circles, smooth with spatula. Bake in very slow oven about 1 hour or until dry; cool in oven with door ajar.

Make up remaining mixture as before, spoon half the meringue into piping bag fitted with 2cm tube, pipe inside remaining marked circle and bake as before.

Spoon remaining mixture into piping bag fitted with 1cm tube, pipe into 30cm lengths onto remaining oven tray. Bake in very slow oven about 30 minutes or until dry to touch. Cut lengths into 6cm pieces while still warm; cool.

Place 1 meringue circle on serving plate, spread with one-third of the mousse filling, repeat layers with remaining meringue circles and mousse filling, ending with a mousse layer. Refrigerate several hours or overnight.

Just before serving, decorate top of cake with lengths of meringue and chocolate lace; sprinkle with sifted icing sugar, if desired.

Mousse Filling: Spread nuts on oven tray, toast in moderate oven about 5 minutes; cool. Sprinkle gelatine over water in cup, stand in small pan of simmering water, stir until dissolved; cool to room temperature.

Combine nuts, gelatine mixture, chocolate, egg yolks and brandy in large bowl; cool to room temperature.

Beat cream until soft peaks form, fold into chocolate mixture in 2 batches. Cover, refrigerate until firm.

Chocolate Lace: Spoon chocolate into piping bag fitted with fine plain tube, drizzle in lacy pattern over piece of baking paper or foil. Allow to set at room temperature; break into pieces.

■ Meringue circles and mousse best assembled a day before serving. Meringue circles and lengths and chocolate lace can be made 2 days ahead. Mousse can be made a day ahead.

■ Storage: Meringue circles and lengths and chocolate lace, in airtight containers. Assembled meringue circles and mousse, covered, in refrigerator.

■ Freeze: Not suitable.

■ Microwave: Gelatine suitable.

ABOVE: Rich Chocolate Meringue and Mousse Cake.

Slimmers' Delight

Serves 6

Tomato and Mussel Soup
Wholemeal Dinner Rolls
chilled dry sherry

**Fillets of Whiting with
Potato Scales**
**Steamed Baby Squash
with Balsamic Vinaigrette**

sauvignon blanc

**Bananas with Grapefruit
and Spiced Ricotta**
medium dry sparkling wine

Every course is light, fresh and satisfying, so your guests will feel indulged but not guilty. The star is seafood, beginning with tomato and mussel soup and home-made rolls; start the soup a day ahead but make the rolls on day of serving. In the main course, we've marinated fish overnight, layered it with potatoes and baked it just before serving with freshly steamed baby squash. Also baked just before serving are honeyed bananas served with grapefruit, grapefruit glaze and do-ahead creamy cheese accompaniment.

TOMATO AND MUSSEL SOUP

20g butter
1 clove garlic, crushed
1 large (about 200g) onion, finely
    chopped
1 medium (about 350g) leek, sliced
1 large (about 180g) carrot, finely
    chopped
1.5kg tomatoes, peeled, seeded
1 bay leaf
1 teaspoon chopped fresh thyme
750g mussels
½ cup water

FISH STOCK
1kg white fish bones
2 litres (8 cups) water
1 medium (about 150g) onion,
    chopped
1 medium (about 120g) carrot,
    chopped
½ stick celery, chopped
4 fresh parsley stems
1 tablespoon black peppercorns

Heat butter in pan, add garlic, onion, leek and carrot, cook, covered, over low heat about 20 minutes or until onion is very soft, stir occasionally. Add chopped tomatoes, bay leaf and thyme, cook, covered, 20 minutes. Add 3 cups of the fish stock, simmer, covered, 10 minutes.

Meanwhile, scrub mussels, remove beards. Heat water in large pan, add mussels, cook, covered, about 5 minutes or until mussels open. Drain mussels; discard liquid, remove mussels from shells; discard shells.

Discard bay leaf from soup, add mussels to soup, stir until heated through.

Fish Stock: Combine all ingredients in large pan, simmer, uncovered, 40 minutes. Strain stock into bowl, discard onion mixture. You will need 3 cups of stock for this recipe; any remaining stock can be frozen for another use.

- Soup can be prepared a day ahead. Add mussels just before serving.
- Storage: Covered, in refrigerator.
- Freeze: Not suitable.
- Microwave: Not suitable.

WHOLEMEAL DINNER ROLLS

1 teaspoon dried yeast
½ teaspoon sugar
½ cup warm water
¼ cup pearl barley
1 cup wholemeal plain flour
1¼ cups white plain flour
1 tablespoon kibbled rye
1 teaspoon fine sea salt
2 tablespoons skim milk powder
⅓ cup warm skim milk

Combine yeast, sugar and water in bowl, cover, stand in warm place about 15 minutes or until frothy. Add barley to pan of boiling water, boil, uncovered, about 10 minutes or until tender, drain.

Sift flours into bowl, return husks to bowl. Stir in barley, rye, salt and milk powder. Stir in yeast mixture and warm milk, mix to a firm dough. Turn dough onto floured surface, knead about 5 minutes or until dough is elastic. Return dough to large greased bowl, cover with greased plastic wrap, stand in warm place about

1 hour or until dough is doubled in size.

Turn dough onto lightly floured surface, knead until smooth. Divide dough into 6 portions, roll each portion into 24cm long oval shape, roll up from short end. Place rolls end to end in greased 26cm x 32cm Swiss roll pan, cover with greased plastic wrap, stand in warm place about 20 minutes or until dough is risen slightly. Brush tops of rolls with a little extra skim milk, bake in moderately hot oven about 20 minutes or until rolls are lightly browned and sound hollow when tapped.

■ Recipe best made on day of serving.
■ Freeze: Suitable.
■ Microwave: Not suitable.

LEFT: Tomato and Mussel Soup with Wholemeal Dinner Rolls.
ABOVE: Fillets of Whiting with Potato Scales and Steamed Baby Squash with Balsamic Vinaigrette.

FILLETS OF WHITING WITH POTATO SCALES

6 (about 720g) whiting fillets
10 (about 650g) baby new potatoes

MARINADE
¼ cup olive oil
2 cloves garlic, crushed
1 teaspoon cracked black peppercorns
2 tablespoons lemon juice
2 teaspoons chopped fresh dill

Remove skin from fish. Place fish in shallow dish, pour over marinade, cover, refrigerate several hours or overnight.

Cut potatoes into 1mm slices. Drain fish from marinade; reserve marinade. Pat top side of fish dry with absorbent paper. Place fish on oven tray, overlap potato slices on top side of fish. Drizzle reserved marinade over potato scales. Bake fish, uncovered, in moderately hot oven about 25 minutes or until tender.

Marinade: Combine all ingredients in bowl; mix well.

■ Fish can be marinated a day ahead. Potatoes best sliced just before cooking.
■ Storage: Fish, covered, in refrigerator.
■ Freeze: Uncooked marinated fish suitable.
■ Microwave: Suitable.

STEAMED BABY SQUASH WITH BALSAMIC VINAIGRETTE

350g baby yellow squash
350g baby green squash
¼ cup balsamic vinegar
½ cup olive oil

Boil, steam or microwave squash until tender, rinse under cold water; drain. Toss in combined vinegar and oil.

■ Recipe best made just before serving.
■ Freeze: Not suitable.
■ Microwave: Suitable.

BANANAS WITH GRAPEFRUIT AND SPICED RICOTTA

3 medium (about 900g) grapefruit
1 tablespoon honey
1 tablespoon brown sugar
¼ teaspoon ground cinnamon
6 medium (about 900g) bananas

GRAPEFRUIT GLAZE
1 cup grapefruit juice
¼ cup lime juice
¼ cup orange juice
2 tablespoons honey
2 tablespoons dark rum
2 teaspoons cornflour
2 teaspoons water

SPICED RICOTTA
1¼ cups (about 280g) low fat
    ricotta cheese
½ teaspoon ground ginger
1 tablespoon honey
2 tablespoons cream
¼ cup pecans, chopped

Peel grapefruit, cut between membranes into segments, remove seeds and any remaining pith; reserve any juice for grapefruit glaze.

Combine honey, sugar and cinnamon in pan, stir over heat, without boiling, until sugar is dissolved; cool 5 minutes. Place bananas on oven tray, brush bananas with honey mixture. Bake, uncovered, in hot oven about 15 minutes or until bananas are soft and lightly browned.

Place sliced bananas and grapefruit on serving plates, serve with grapefruit glaze and spiced ricotta.

Grapefruit Glaze: Including any reserved juice, combine strained juices, honey and rum in pan, bring to boil, add blended cornflour and water, stir over heat until mixture boils and thickens slightly.

Spiced Ricotta: Combine all ingredients in small bowl; mix well.

■ Bananas and grapefruit glaze best made just before serving. Grapefruit best prepared just before serving. Spiced ricotta can be made several hours ahead.

■ Storage: Spiced ricotta, covered, in refrigerator.

■ Freeze: Not suitable.

■ Microwave: Not suitable.

LEFT: Bananas with Grapefruit and Spiced Ricotta.

China from Wedgwood; cutlery from Noritake; linen from Butler & Co.; service plates, Alessi bowl, place name and oil server from Bibelot.

Fast and Fabulous

Serves 8

Roasted Garlic Dip with Bagel Croutons

dry white riesling or chablis

Seared Beef Salad with Lime Dressing

Crispy Noodles

rosé

Macerated Pineapple

Fresh Mint Ice-Cream

mint liqueur

Take a relaxing break from lots of cooking with this cool menu. Quickly baked bagel slices are served with the garlic dip; roasting the garlic takes a little while, but is straightforward. For the very tasty salad, simply pan-fry the beef, slice it and marinate slices in the spicy dressing, ready to assemble with salad; noodles can be deep-fried about an hour ahead. At least a week ahead, you could make the lovely ice-cream, refreshing with pineapple macerated overnight in minty rum mixture.

Trim beef. Heat oil in pan, add beef, cook until well browned all over and cooked as desired; cool. Slice beef thinly. Pour ⅓ cup of the dressing over beef in bowl, cover, refrigerate several hours or overnight.

Add asparagus to pan of boiling water, boil, uncovered, 1 minute, add snow peas, return to boil. Drain immediately, rinse under cold water; drain.

Combine spinach leaves with remaining ingredients in large bowl. Stir in undrained beef, asparagus, peas and remaining dressing.

Lime Dressing: Combine all ingredients in bowl; mix well.

- Beef can be prepared a day ahead. Salad can be made 3 hours ahead.
- Storage: Covered, in refrigerator.
- Freeze: Not suitable.
- Microwave: Asparagus and snow peas suitable.

LEFT: Roasted Garlic Dip with Bagel Croutons.
BELOW: Seared Beef Salad with Crispy Noodles.
RIGHT: Macerated Pineapple with Fresh Mint Ice-Cream.

ROASTED GARLIC DIP WITH BAGEL CROUTONS

8 medium (about 560g) garlic bulbs
¼ cup olive oil
½ cup water
2 tablespoons olive oil, extra

BAGEL CROUTONS
6 bagels, thinly sliced
½ cup olive oil
¾ cup (185g) sun-dried tomato paste

Place garlic bulbs in baking dish, brush with oil, add water. Bake, covered, in moderate oven 40 minutes; uncover, bake about further 45 minutes or until garlic is soft; cool. Squeeze pulp from cloves into bowl, stir in extra oil. Serve roasted garlic dip with bagel croutons.

Bagel Croutons: Brush bagel slices with combined oil and paste, place on wire racks over oven trays. Bake in moderate oven about 5 minutes or until crisp.

- Recipe can be made a day ahead.
- Storage: Croutons, in airtight container. Dip, covered, in refrigerator.
- Freeze: Croutons suitable.
- Microwave: Not suitable.

SEARED BEEF SALAD

1.5kg beef rump steak
2 tablespoons oil
2 bunches (about 500g) fresh asparagus spears, chopped
200g snow peas
1 bunch (about 650g) English spinach
4 cups (300g) bean sprouts
1 medium (about 170g) red Spanish onion, sliced
1 medium (about 200g) red pepper, thinly sliced
2 medium (about 240g) carrots, thinly sliced
8 medium (about 120g) radishes, quartered

LIME DRESSING
1 cup oil
¾ cup lime juice
¼ cup chopped fresh coriander
2 tablespoons chopped fresh lemon grass
3 teaspoons sambal oelek
2 tablespoons fish sauce
1½ tablespoons sugar
3 cloves garlic, crushed
1 tablespoon chopped fresh mint
1 tablespoon sesame seeds, toasted

CRISPY NOODLES

250g rice vermicelli
oil for deep-frying

Add vermicelli to hot oil in batches. When vermicelli puffs and rises to the surface, remove with slotted spoon. Drain on absorbent paper.

- Recipe can be made an hour ahead.
- Freeze: Not suitable.
- Microwave: Not suitable.

MACERATED PINEAPPLE

1 medium (about 1.25kg) pineapple
1 cup pineapple juice, approximately
⅓ cup castor sugar
1½ tablespoons dark rum
2 tablespoons shredded fresh mint

Cut peeled pineapple in half lengthways, cut each half into 5mm slices (you will need 24 slices). Place slices into bowl.

Blend or process any remaining pineapple, measure pineapple puree, make up to 1½ cups with juice. Combine juice mixture and sugar in pan, stir over heat, without boiling, until sugar is dissolved. Simmer, without stirring, about

3 minutes or until mixture reduces by one-third; cool 5 minutes. Stir in rum and mint, pour over pineapple, cover, refrigerate several hours or overnight. Serve pineapple drizzled with syrup. Serve with fresh mint ice-cream.

- Recipe best made a day ahead.
- Storage: Covered, in refrigerator.
- Freeze: Not suitable.
- Microwave: Not suitable.

FRESH MINT ICE-CREAM

1¼ cups castor sugar
1¼ cups water
⅔ cup fresh mint leaves
⅓ cup lime juice
600ml carton thickened cream, whipped

Combine sugar and water in pan, stir over heat, without boiling, until sugar is dissolved. Simmer 5 minutes, without stirring, cool 5 minutes. Blend or process syrup with mint and juice. Strain through fine nylon sieve (to prevent mint discolouring); discard mint. Pour mixture into shallow pan, cover, freeze until firm.

Process ice-cream mixture until smooth, transfer to bowl, fold in cream in several batches. Return to same pan, cover, freeze until firm. Repeat processing, spread into loaf pan, cover, freeze several hours or overnight until firm.

- Recipe best made several days ahead.
- Storage: Covered, in freezer.
- Freeze: Essential.
- Microwave: Not suitable.

Formal Celebration

Serves 20

Mini Spinach and Red Pepper Roulades
dry sparkling wine

❦

Marinated Scallops with Pancetta and Olives
sauvignon blanc

❦

Fillet of Beef with Pepper Crust
Potatoes with Sun-Dried Tomatoes and Basil
Beans in Chive Butter
medium-bodied cabernet sauvignon

❦

Cheese Platter with Figs and Raisin Toast
cabernet sauvignon

❦

Coffee Hazelnut Ice-Cream Gateau
dry sparkling wine

❦

Whether it's a 21st birthday, anniversary or any red-letter day, our
menu is both stylish and surprisingly simple. The roulades, scallops
and potatoes can be prepared ahead, and the ice-cream gateau
goes into the freezer. Allow around 1½ hours for the beef if serving
hot, then last-minute finishing includes scallops, gravy, beans and
cheese platter. If you prefer, serve the whole meal cold.

MINI SPINACH AND RED PEPPER ROULADES

SPINACH ROULADE
1 bunch (about 650g) English
    spinach, finely shredded
60g butter
3 green shallots, chopped
⅓ cup plain flour
1 cup milk
3 eggs, separated
10 slices (about 200g) smoked
    salmon
¼ cup sour cream
fresh dill sprigs

RED PEPPER ROULADE
1 medium (about 200g) red pepper
60g butter
⅓ cup plain flour
1 cup milk
3 eggs, separated
2 tablespoons grated parmesan
    cheese
1½ tablespoons olive paste

Spinach Roulade: Lightly grease 26cm x 32cm Swiss roll pan, cover base with paper; grease paper. Boil, steam or microwave spinach until tender; drain, squeeze well to remove excess liquid.

Heat butter in pan, add shallots, stir over heat until soft. Stir in flour, stir over heat until bubbling. Remove from heat, gradually stir in milk, then stir over heat until mixture boils and thickens. Stir in spinach and egg yolks; transfer mixture to large bowl.

Beat egg whites in small bowl with electric mixer until soft peaks form, fold into spinach mixture in 2 batches. Spread into prepared pan, bake in hot oven about 12 minutes or until puffed and lightly browned.

Turn onto wire rack covered with tea-towel. Carefully remove paper, cut roulade base in half lengthways; cool. Top each half with salmon, roll up from long side to enclose salmon, wrap in plastic wrap; refrigerate 1 hour or until required.

Just before serving, cut roulades into 1cm slices, top with sour cream and dill.

Red Pepper Roulade: Lightly grease 26cm x 32cm Swiss roll pan, cover base with paper; grease paper.

Quarter pepper, remove seeds and membrane. Grill pepper, skin side up, until skin blisters and blackens. Peel away skin; discard skin. Blend or process pepper until smooth. You will need ¼ cup pepper puree for this recipe.

Heat butter in pan, stir in flour, stir over heat until bubbling. Remove from heat, gradually stir in milk, stir over heat until mixture boils and thickens. Stir in pepper puree, egg yolks and cheese, transfer to large bowl.

Beat egg whites in small bowl with electric mixer until soft peaks form, fold into pepper mixture. Spread into prepared pan, bake in hot oven about 12 minutes or until puffed and lightly browned. Turn onto

wire rack covered with tea-towel. Carefully remove paper, cut roulade base in half lengthways; cool. Spread each half with olive paste, roll up from long side to enclose paste, wrap in plastic wrap; refrigerate 1 hour or until required. Cut roulades into 1cm slices.

Makes about 60.

■ Roulades can be made a day ahead.
■ Storage: Covered, in refrigerator.
■ Freeze: Not suitable.
■ Microwave: Spinach suitable.

ABOVE: Mini Spinach and Red Pepper Roulades.
RIGHT: Marinated Scallops with Pancetta and Olives.

MARINATED SCALLOPS WITH PANCETTA AND OLIVES

We used scallops from Coffin Bay, South Australia, in this recipe. The colourful shells are ideal for serving.

60 scallops in shells
1 tablespoon olive oil
20 slices (about 360g) pancetta
1 large mignonette lettuce
½ bunch curly endive
160g snow pea sprouts
1 medium (about 200g) green pepper, sliced
250g pimiento-stuffed green olives, drained, halved

DRESSING
1 cup olive oil
½ cup lemon juice
2 tablespoons balsamic vinegar
2 tablespoons chopped fresh coriander
1 clove garlic, crushed
2 teaspoons honey

Remove scallops from shells; cut through muscle that attaches the scallop to the shell; trim away veins from scallops.

Add shells to pan of boiling water, remove any remaining scallop from shells and dry shells well.

Heat oil in heavy-based pan, add scallops, cook until browned on both sides and tender. Place scallops into bowl, stir in dressing; cover; refrigerate several hours or overnight.

Cut pancetta into thin strips, grill until crisp; cool. Tear lettuce and endive into pieces. Drain scallops; reserve dressing.

Just before serving, place scallops in shells on serving plates. Serve with combined lettuce, endive, sprouts, pepper and olives; drizzle with any remaining dressing; sprinkle with pancetta.

Dressing: Combine all ingredients in jar; shake well.

■ Scallops can be marinated a day ahead.
■ Storage: Covered, in refrigerator.
■ Freeze: Not suitable.
■ Microwave: Not suitable.

FILLET OF BEEF WITH PEPPER CRUST

2 x 2kg pieces beef scotch fillet
⅓ cup oil

PEPPER CRUST
⅓ cup French mustard
2½ cups (175g) stale breadcrumbs
½ cup seasoned pepper
¼ cup chopped fresh parsley
2 eggs, lightly beaten
1 teaspoon garlic powder
¼ cup dry white wine
30g butter, melted

GRAVY
⅓ cup plain flour
2 cups dry red wine
3 cups beef stock
2 tablespoons Worcestershire sauce

Trim excess fat from beef, tie beef with string at 2cm intervals. Heat oil in 2 baking dishes. Add beef, brown all over; cool.

Press pepper crust over beef. Bake in moderate oven about 1 hour and 10 minutes or until cooked as desired. Remove from dish, keep warm; reserve ⅓ cup juices in dish for gravy. Remove crust from beef. Serve beef sliced with pieces of crust and gravy. Serve with potatoes with sun-dried tomatoes and basil, and beans in chive butter. Beef can also be served cold, if desired. If serving cold, omit gravy.

Pepper Crust: Combine all ingredients in bowl; mix well.

Gravy: Heat reserved juices in pan, stir in flour, stir over heat until bubbling. Remove from heat, gradually stir in wine, stock and sauce, stir over heat until mixture boils and thickens; strain.

- Beef can be prepared a day ahead. Gravy best made just before serving.
- Storage: Covered, in refrigerator.
- Freeze: Not suitable.
- Microwave: Not suitable.

POTATOES WITH SUN-DRIED TOMATOES AND BASIL

10 large (about 2kg) potatoes
2 tablespoons olive oil
4 medium (about 1.4kg) leeks, sliced
2 cloves garlic, crushed
1 cup (185g) drained sun-dried
  tomatoes, sliced
½ cup shredded fresh basil
600ml carton thickened cream
⅓ cup milk
1 cup (80g) grated parmesan cheese
½ teaspoon paprika

Grease baking dish (14 cup capacity). Thinly slice potatoes. Heat oil in pan, add leeks and garlic, cook, stirring, until leeks are very soft. Remove from heat; stir in tomatoes and basil.

Spread half the potato into prepared dish, top with leek mixture; top with remaining potato. Pour combined cream and milk over potato, sprinkle with com-

bined cheese and paprika. Bake, uncovered, in moderate oven about 2 hours or until potato is tender.

If you make this dish a day ahead, it will take about 20 minutes, covered, in a moderate oven to reheat. This can also be served cold, if desired.

- Recipe can be made a day ahead.
- Storage: Covered, in refrigerator.
- Freeze: Suitable.
- Microwave: Not suitable.

BEANS IN CHIVE BUTTER

1kg green beans, halved
1kg butter beans, halved
½ cup pine nuts, toasted
125g butter, melted
¼ cup chopped fresh chives
1 clove garlic, crushed

Boil, steam or microwave beans until tender; drain.

If serving beans hot, toss beans in combined nuts, butter, chives and garlic.

If serving beans cold, omit butter and toss beans in combined nuts, a little salad dressing, chives and garlic.

- Beans with butter are best made just before serving. Beans with salad dressing can be made a day ahead.
- Storage: Covered, in refrigerator.
- Freeze: Not suitable.
- Microwave: Suitable.

LEFT: Fillet of Beef with Pepper Crust, Beans in Chive Butter, and Potatoes with Sun-Dried Tomatoes and Basil.

CHEESE PLATTER WITH FIGS AND RAISIN TOAST

600g brie cheese
600g blue cheese
2 tablespoons balsamic vinegar
⅓ cup olive oil
1 bunch watercress
2 bunches rocket
10 medium (about 2kg) fresh figs, halved
1 loaf raisin bread, toasted

Cut each cheese into 20 portions (about 30g each). Combine vinegar and oil in bowl. Toss watercress and rocket leaves in vinegar and oil mixture. Serve cheese with figs, raisin toast and salad.

■ Recipe best made just before serving.
■ Freeze: Not suitable.

ABOVE: Cheese Platter with Figs and Raisin Toast.
RIGHT AND FAR RIGHT: Coffee Hazelnut Ice-Cream Gateau.

China and glassware from Villeroy & Boch; cutlery from Georg Jensen. Right: silver tray by Stokes; knife by Whitehill Silver.

COFFEE HAZELNUT ICE-CREAM GATEAU

We used a deep 30cm cake ring for this recipe. They are available from specialty kitchen shops. If unavailable, use a deep 30cm cake pan. Freeze left-over egg whites in batches for use in meringues and meringue toppings, etc., if desired. You will need to buy 3 x 300ml cartons cream for this recipe.

½ cup roasted hazelnuts

HAZELNUT ICE-CREAM
10 egg yolks
1 cup castor sugar
3½ cups milk
½ cup castor sugar, extra
1¾ cups cream
¼ cup chocolate hazelnut spread

COFFEE ICE-CREAM
3½ cups milk
1½ cups coffee beans
½ cup castor sugar
10 egg yolks
1 cup castor sugar, extra
1¾ cups cream

CREME ANGLAISE
16 egg yolks
1 cup castor sugar
1½ litres (6 cups) milk
½ cup castor sugar, extra
1 tablespoon vanilla essence
1 tablespoon coffee essence

Lightly oil deep 30cm cake ring, place on lightly oiled tray, place in freezer for 1 hour. Spread hazelnut ice-cream into prepared ring, return to freezer, cover, freeze several hours or until firm. Spread coffee ice-cream over hazelnut ice-cream, decorate with hazelnuts, cover, freeze several hours or overnight.

Run a hot knife around edge of ring and remove. Serve with vanilla and coffee creme anglaise.

Hazelnut Ice-Cream: Whisk egg yolks and sugar in large bowl until thick and creamy. Heat milk and extra sugar in pan, stir over heat until sugar is dissolved, remove from heat.

Gradually whisk milk mixture into yolk mixture, pour back into same pan, stir over low heat, without boiling, until mixture is thickened. Strain into large bowl, stir in cream and chocolate hazelnut spread, mix well; cool. Pour mixture into large cake pan, cover, freeze several hours or until just firm.

Spoon half of the mixture into large bowl, beat with electric mixer until smooth and creamy. Return mixture to large pan. Repeat with remaining mixture, cover, freeze until firm. Beat mixture again before using.

Coffee Ice-Cream: Heat milk, coffee beans and sugar in large pan, bring to boil, remove from heat, cover, stand 1 hour. Strain milk mixture; discard beans. Whisk egg yolks and extra sugar in large bowl until thick and creamy. Whisk milk mixture into yolk mixture. Pour back into same pan, stir over low heat, without boiling, until mixture is thickened. Strain into large bowl, stir in cream, mix well; cool.

Pour mixture into large cake pan, cover, freeze several hours or until just firm. Spoon half of the mixture into large bowl, beat with electric mixer until smooth and creamy. Return mixture to pan. Repeat with remaining mixture, cover, freeze until firm. Beat mixture again before using.

Creme Anglaise: Whisk egg yolks and sugar in large bowl until thick and creamy. Combine milk and extra sugar in large pan, bring to boil, remove from heat. Whisk milk mixture into yolk mixture. Pour back into same pan, stir over low heat, without boiling, until mixture thickens slightly. Strain mixture, divide into 2 bowls. Stir vanilla essence into 1 bowl, cover, cool. Stir coffee essence in other bowl, cover, cool. Refrigerate until required.

- Ice-cream gateau can be made a week ahead. Creme anglaise can be made 2 days ahead.
- Storage: Gateau, covered, in freezer. Creme anglaise, covered, in refrigerator.
- Freeze: Gateau essential. Creme anglaise not suitable.
- Microwave: Not suitable.

Casual Do-Ahead Buffet

Serves 12

Mini Crab Cakes with Red Pepper Sauce
gewurztraminer

❦

Egg Mayonnaise with Pizza Toppings
medium dry riesling

❦

Beef Casserole with Baby Mushrooms
Buttered Rice with Vegetables
Spinach and Avocado Salad
cabernet sauvignon

❦

Caramel Apple Tart
sauternes-style white wine

❦

Our wintry-style buffet menu is a great way to entertain a lot of people when you can't give a sit-down, formal meal. You simply set out all the food and let guests help themselves. It's all eaten with a fork, and most can be prepared ahead. Then, just before serving, deep-fry the crab cakes, finish the beef casserole, reheat the rice, slice the avocados and assemble the salad. You'll want whipped cream, too, for the luscious, already-made caramel apple tart.

MINI CRAB CAKES WITH RED PEPPER SAUCE

4 x 170g cans crab, drained
5 green shallots, chopped
2 teaspoons grated lemon rind
2 cloves garlic, crushed
2 teaspoons chopped fresh dill
1½ cups (about 110g) stale
    breadcrumbs
½ cup milk
3 eggs, lightly beaten
oil for deep-frying

RED PEPPER SAUCE
4 medium (about 800g) red peppers
½ cup sour cream
1 clove garlic, crushed
¼ teaspoon sugar

Combine crab, shallots, rind, garlic, dill and breadcrumbs in bowl, stir in combined milk and eggs. Flatten tablespoons of mixture into patties.

Deep-fry patties in hot oil until lightly browned; drain on absorbent paper. Serve mini crab cakes warm or cold with red pepper sauce.

Red Pepper Sauce: Quarter peppers, remove seeds and membranes. Grill peppers, skin side up, until skin blisters and blackens, peel away skin. Blend or process peppers; you will need 1 cup puree for this recipe. Stir in sour cream, garlic and sugar.

- Recipe can be made several hours ahead.
- Storage: Covered, in refrigerator.
- Freeze: Not suitable.
- Microwave: Not suitable.

EGG MAYONNAISE WITH PIZZA TOPPINGS

24 hard-boiled eggs, chopped
300g carton sour cream
1 cup mayonnaise
5 green shallots, chopped
1⅓ cups (about 240g) black olives,
    chopped
125g prosciutto, shredded
½ cup shredded fresh basil
2 tablespoons chopped fresh
    flat-leafed parsley
2 x 45g can anchovy fillets, drained,
    chopped
¾ cup drained sun-dried tomatoes,
    sliced
½ cup drained sliced sun-dried
    zucchini

GARLIC FOCACCIA
3 x 16cm x 19cm pieces of focaccia
4 cloves garlic, crushed
250g butter, melted

LEFT: Mini Crab Cakes with Red Pepper Sauce.
ABOVE: Egg Mayonnaise with Pizza Toppings.

BEEF CASSEROLE WITH BABY MUSHROOMS

2.5kg chuck steak
8 bacon rashers, chopped
¾ cup oil
24 baby (about 600g) onions
4 cloves garlic, crushed
1¾ cups dry red wine
⅔ cup tomato paste
2½ cups beef stock
500g baby mushrooms
1 small fresh red chilli, chopped
2 tablespoons chopped fresh tarragon

Cut steak into 2cm cubes. Cook bacon in pan until crisp; drain on absorbent paper. Heat ¼ cup of the oil in pan, add onions and garlic, cook, stirring, until onions are lightly browned; remove from pan. Heat remaining oil in pan, add steak in batches, cook, stirring, until well browned all over. Return steak to pan with any juices, stir in wine, tomato paste and stock, simmer, covered, 45 minutes. Stir in onion mixture, simmer, covered, 30 minutes.

Just before serving, stir in mushrooms and chilli, simmer, covered, further 15 minutes or until steak is tender. Stir in bacon and tarragon. Serve beef casserole with buttered rice with vegetables and spinach and avocado salad.

- Casserole can be made a day ahead.
- Storage: Covered, in refrigerator.
- Freeze: Suitable without mushrooms.
- Microwave: Not suitable.

Combine eggs, sour cream, mayonnaise and shallots in bowl. Spread a 2cm layer of egg mixture over large platter. Sprinkle olives in a row over quarter of the egg mixture. Arrange prosciutto over next quarter. Add combined basil, parsley and anchovies to next quarter. Place combined tomatoes and zucchini over remaining quarter of egg mixture. Serve egg mayonnaise platter with garlic focaccia.

Garlic Focaccia: Cut focaccia into 1cm strips, cut each strip into 8cm fingers. Combine garlic and butter in bowl. Brush garlic butter on each side of focaccia fingers, place on oven tray in single layer, bake in moderately hot oven about 12 minutes or until lightly browned and crisp.

- Recipe can be prepared several hours ahead.
- Storage: Egg mayonnaise, covered, in refrigerator. Focaccia: In airtight container.
- Freeze: Not suitable.
- Microwave: Not suitable.

RIGHT: Beef Casserole with Baby Mushrooms.

BUTTERED RICE WITH VEGETABLES

3 cups (600g) brown rice
3 cups (600g) white rice
125g butter
6 green shallots, chopped
4 cloves garlic, crushed
2 large (about 360g) carrots, diced
1 medium (about 200g) green pepper,
finely chopped
2 medium (about 200g) zucchini,
finely chopped
440g can corn kernels, drained
2 tablespoons chopped fresh basil

Add brown rice to large pan of boiling water, boil, uncovered, until just tender; drain. Repeat with white rice.

Heat butter in pan, add shallots and garlic, cook, stirring, until shallots are soft. Stir in carrots, pepper, zucchini and corn, cook, stirring, until vegetables are just tender; stir in basil. Combine vegetable mixture and rice in large bowl.

Just before serving, return rice to pan in batches, stir until heated through.

- Recipe can be prepared a day ahead.
- Storage: Covered, in refrigerator.
- Freeze: Rice suitable.
- Microwave: Suitable.

SPINACH AND AVOCADO SALAD

1 bunch (about 650g) English spinach
2 butter lettuce
1 green oak leaf lettuce
3 medium (about 750g) avocados,
sliced
1 cup (80g) parmesan cheese flakes

DRESSING
1¼ cups olive oil
⅓ cup lemon juice
3 cloves garlic, crushed
1 teaspoon sugar

Tear spinach and lettuce into pieces. Combine all ingredients in large bowl. Add dressing, toss lightly to combine.
Dressing: Combine all ingredients in jar; shake well.

- Recipe best made just before serving. Dressing can be made 2 days ahead.
- Storage: Dressing, covered, in refrigerator.
- Freeze: Not suitable.

CARAMEL APPLE TART

2 cups plain flour
½ cup self-raising flour
⅓ cup cornflour
⅓ cup icing sugar
250g butter, chopped
⅓ cup water, approximately

APPLE PUREE
6 medium (about 1kg) apples
2 tablespoons water
½ cinnamon stick
¼ teaspoon ground allspice
2 tablespoons castor sugar
pinch ground cloves

APPLES AND CARAMEL CUSTARD
4 medium (about 600g) apples
80g butter
⅔ cup brown sugar
2 tablespoons hot water
300ml carton cream
3 eggs, lightly beaten

Sift flours and icing sugar into bowl, rub in butter. Add enough water to make ingredients cling together, press dough into a ball, knead lightly on floured surface until smooth. Divide dough in half, cover, refrigerate 30 minutes.

Roll half the dough on lightly floured surface until large enough to line 23cm flan tin, trim edges. Cover pastry with paper, fill with dried beans or rice. Bake in moderately hot oven 10 minutes. Remove paper and beans, bake about further 10 minutes or until lightly browned; cool. Repeat with remaining pastry.

Spoon half the apple puree into 1 pastry case, top with half the apples, pour over half the caramel custard. Repeat with remaining pastry case, puree, apples and custard. Bake in moderate oven about 45 minutes or until custard is set; cool.

Apple Puree: Peel, core and quarter apples. Place apples in pan with remaining ingredients, cover, cook for about 15 minutes or until apples are soft. Discard cinnamon stick. Blend or process apple mixture until smooth, cool.

Apples and Caramel Custard: Peel, core and quarter apples. Make lengthways cuts into rounded sides of apple quarters, cutting about three-quarters of the way through. Combine butter, sugar and water in pan, stir over heat, without boiling, until butter is melted and sugar dissolved. Add apple quarters, coat apples in syrup, simmer, uncovered,

about 30 minutes or until apples are soft. Remove apples, place on wire rack to cool, pat dry. Cool caramel slightly, whisk in combined cream and eggs.

Makes 2.

- Recipe can be made several hours ahead. Pastry shells and puree can be made a day ahead.
- Storage: Pastry shells, in airtight container. Puree, covered, in refrigerator.
- Freeze: Not suitable.
- Microwave: Not suitable.

FAR LEFT: Buttered Rice with Vegetables, Spinach and Avocado Salad.
ABOVE: Caramel Apple Tart.

China and glassware from Villeroy & Boch; ice bucket from Strachan.

Old-Fashioned Favourites

Serves 6

Chicken Liver Pate with Cranberry Compote
late-picked riesling

❧

Roast Pork with Apple Seasoning
Baked Potatoes, Kumara and Onions
Saute Brussels Sprouts
full-bodied cabernet sauvignon

❧

Steamed Ginger Puddings with all the Trimmings
sweet sparkling wine

❧

A wonderful roast dinner like this makes us think instantly of warmth, comfort, home and family, and how much guests enjoyed it, too. The pate and cranberry compote are an easy do-ahead start, but allow about 2 hours for roasting the seasoned pork, making the sauce and cooking the vegetables (those crispy potatoes are a treat)! About the same time, steam the little ginger puddings; these, crowned with caramelised glace ginger, are eaten with luscious accompaniments all ready to assemble.

CHICKEN LIVER PATE WITH CRANBERRY COMPOTE

30g butter
1 tablespoon oil
1 small (about 80g) onion, chopped
2 cloves garlic, crushed
750g chicken livers
2 tablespoons chopped fresh thyme
½ cup port
⅓ cup chicken stock
300g soft butter, extra
1 teaspoon gelatine
½ cup chicken stock, extra
1 tablespoon drained green
    peppercorns

CRANBERRY COMPOTE
250g frozen cranberries
¼ cup sugar
1 teaspoon grated orange rind
1 tablespoon orange juice
1½ tablespoons dry red wine

MELBA TOAST
¾ loaf unsliced white bread

Heat butter and oil in large heavy-based pan, add onion and garlic, cook, stirring, until onion is soft. Add livers and thyme, cook over high heat about 3 minutes or until livers are browned but still pink inside. Transfer livers to processor.

Add port and stock to same pan, simmer until reduced by half, pour over livers, process until smooth. With processor operating, add extra butter a small piece at a time, process until smooth. Push pate through sieve, spoon into 6 moulds (½ cup capacity), cover, refrigerate until pate is firm.

Sprinkle gelatine over extra stock in cup, stand in small pan of simmering water, stir until dissolved. Sprinkle peppercorns over pate, carefully pour gelatine mixture over pate, refrigerate until firm. Serve pate with cranberry compote and melba toast.

Cranberry Compote: Combine all ingredients in pan, simmer about 10 minutes or until thick, stirring occasionally.

Melba Toast: Remove crusts from bread, cut bread in half diagonally to form 2 large triangles. Cut triangles into very thin slices, place on oven trays. Bake in moderately slow oven about 10 minutes or until crisp and lightly browned; turn during cooking.

- Pate and compote can be prepared 2 days ahead; Melba toast can be made a week ahead.
- Storage: Pate and compote, covered, in refrigerator. Melba toast, in airtight container.
- Freeze: Not suitable.
- Microwave: Compote suitable.

LEFT: Chicken Liver Pate with Cranberry Compote.

RIGHT: Roast Pork with Apple Seasoning, Baked Potatoes, Kumara and Onions, and Saute Brussels Sprouts.

ROAST PORK WITH APPLE SEASONING

²⁄₃ cup pitted prunes, halved
1 cup dry red wine
1.5kg boned loin of pork
1 tablespoon oil
1 teaspoon salt
2 tablespoons plain flour
1½ cups beef stock

APPLE SEASONING
30g butter
1 teaspoon oil
1 medium (about 150g) onion, chopped
2 cloves garlic, crushed
1 stick celery, finely chopped
1 medium (about 150g) apple, finely chopped
1 tablespoon grated lemon rind
1 tablespoon chopped fresh thyme
1 tablespoon chopped fresh sage
¼ cup chopped walnuts
1 teaspoon prepared horseradish
3½ cups (250g) stale breadcrumbs
1 egg, lightly beaten

Combine prunes and wine in bowl, cover, stand several hours or overnight.

Score rind of pork with cuts about 2cm apart. Place pork on bench with rind side down. Make a cut down centre of pork lengthways, without cutting through. Cut evenly from centre to 1 side of pork to create a flap. Repeat on other side.

Place flaps out to sides of pork, spoon seasoning along centre of pork, roll up firmly, secure with string at 2cm intervals. Rub oil and salt into rind.

Place pork on wire rack in baking dish, bake, uncovered, in hot oven about 10 minutes or until rind begins to crackle. Reduce heat to moderate, bake about further 1½ hours or until tender.

Remove pork from baking dish; keep warm. Drain prunes, reserve wine. Discard all but 2 tablespoons of juices from dish, stir flour into dish, stir over heat until bubbling. Remove from heat, gradually stir in reserved wine and stock, stir over heat until sauce boils and thickens. Strain sauce, return to heat. Stir in prunes, simmer 2 minutes. Serve sauce over sliced pork. Serve with baked potatoes, kumara and onions and saute brussels sprouts.

Apple Seasoning: Heat butter and oil in pan, add onion, garlic and celery, cook, stirring, until onion is soft. Stir in apple, rind and herbs, cook until apple is just soft. Transfer mixture to bowl, stir in remaining ingredients.

- ■ Recipe best prepared on day of serving.
- ■ Freeze: Not suitable.
- ■ Microwave: Not suitable.

BAKED POTATOES, KUMARA AND ONIONS

4 large (about 800g) potatoes
1 medium (about 400g) kumara
3 medium (about 450g) onions
oil

Cut potatoes and kumara into wedges about 2cm thick. Peel onions, leaving root attached at base; cut each onion into quarters through root. Rub vegetables with oil, place on wire rack in baking dish. Bake in moderately hot oven about 40 minutes or until vegetables are tender and browned; turn once during cooking.

- ■ Bake vegetables just before serving.
- ■ Freeze: Not suitable.
- ■ Microwave: Not suitable.

SAUTE BRUSSELS SPROUTS

500g brussels sprouts
60g butter

Boil, steam or microwave sprouts until just tender; drain. Heat butter in pan, add sprouts, stir over high heat until sprouts are heated through.

- ■ Recipe best made just before serving.
- ■ Storage: Covered, in refrigerator.
- ■ Freeze: Suitable.
- ■ Microwave: Suitable.

STEAMED GINGER PUDDINGS WITH ALL THE TRIMMINGS

⅓ cup brown sugar
1½ tablespoons water
2 teaspoons butter
2 tablespoons chopped glace ginger

GINGER PUDDINGS
90g butter
⅓ cup brown sugar
2 eggs
¼ cup plain flour
⅔ cup self-raising flour
1 teaspoon ground cinnamon
1 teaspoon ground ginger
2 tablespoons milk

CINNAMON ICE-CREAM
1 cup milk
300ml carton thickened cream
1 cinnamon stick
¾ teaspoon ground cinnamon
4 egg yolks
½ cup castor sugar

POACHED PEARS
3 firm pears
1 cup castor sugar
2 cups water
1 cinnamon stick

BUTTERSCOTCH SAUCE
50g butter
½ cup brown sugar, firmly packed
300ml carton thickened cream

Grease 6 ovenproof moulds (½ cup capacity). Line base of moulds with rounds of greaseproof paper. Combine sugar, water and butter in pan, stir over heat, without boiling, until sugar is dissolved. Boil about 1 minute or until mixture is slightly thickened. Gently stir in ginger, pour into prepared moulds; top with ginger pudding mixture. Cover moulds with rounds of greased foil.

Place moulds in baking dish with enough boiling water to come halfway up sides of moulds. Bake in moderate oven about 25 minutes or until puddings are cooked. Stand puddings 5 minutes before turning onto serving plates. Serve with cinnamon ice-cream, poached pears and butterscotch sauce.

Ginger Puddings: Beat butter and sugar in small bowl with electric mixer until light and fluffy. Add eggs 1 a time, beating well between additions. Stir in sifted flours and spices and milk in 2 batches.

Cinnamon Ice-Cream: Combine milk, cream, cinnamon stick and ground cinnamon in pan, bring to boil; remove from heat. Cover pan, stand 10 minutes; strain cream mixture, discard cinnamon stick.

Beat egg yolks and sugar in small bowl with electric mixer until thick and creamy, gradually beat in cream mixture. Pour mixture into loaf pan, cover, freeze about 3 hours or until just firm.

Spoon mixture into large bowl, beat with electric mixer until smooth and creamy. Return to pan, cover, repeat freezing and beating once more. Freeze, covered, several hours or overnight.

Poached Pears: Peel pears, cut in half lengthways; remove cores. Combine sugar, water and cinnamon in pan, stir over heat, without boiling, until sugar is dissolved. Add pears to pan, place round of greaseproof paper over pear mixture to prevent pears turning brown. Simmer pears about 15 minutes or until just tender; cool in liquid.

Butterscotch Sauce: Heat butter in pan, add sugar, stir over heat, without boiling, until sugar is dissolved. Add cream, simmer about 5 minutes or until sauce is slightly thickened; serve warm.

■ Puddings best made just before serving. Ice-cream can be made 3 days ahead. Pears and butterscotch sauce can be made 2 days ahead.
■ Storage: Ice-cream, covered, in freezer. Pears and sauce, covered, in refrigerator.
■ Freeze: Ice-cream essential.
■ Microwave: Pears and sauce suitable.

BELOW: Steamed Ginger Puddings with all the Trimmings.

China and glassware from Waterford Wedgwood; cutlery from Wirths; serviettes from Lillywhites; table from Corso di Fiori.

A Feast from the East

Serves 6

Sesame Onion Rolls with Honey Plum Sauce

medium-dry riesling

Prawn and Lemon Grass Salad

young sauvignon blanc
or fume blanc

Citrus Duck with Spicy Ginger Glaze
Saute Bok Choy with Noodles

young sauvignon blanc
or fume blanc

Blueberry Mango Tartlets with Strawberry Sauce

late-picked riesling

Our Asian-inspired menu borrows freely from Thai, Chinese and Indian cuisines, with tastes and textures to delight your palate. It's best to marinate the prawns and duck fillets the day ahead, and nearly everything else can be prepared then, as well. This leaves only a little bit of last-minute cooking for the rolls, prawns, duck and vegetables. The dessert, both pretty and easy, is assembled just before serving.

SESAME ONION ROLLS WITH HONEY PLUM SAUCE

¾ cup plain flour
1 teaspoon turmeric
1 tablespoon sesame seeds, toasted
3 eggs, lightly beaten
1 tablespoon oil
1 cup milk
1 egg, lightly beaten, extra
oil for deep-frying, extra

ONION FILLING
30g butter
1 tablespoon oil
3 medium (about 450g) onions, sliced
3 cloves garlic, crushed
2 teaspoons sugar
1 tablespoon plain flour
1½ tablespoons light soy sauce
⅔ cup chopped fresh chives

HONEY PLUM SAUCE
⅓ cup plum sauce
⅓ cup dry sherry
1 teaspoon honey
2 teaspoons light soy sauce

Sift flour and turmeric into bowl, stir in sesame seeds, gradually stir in combined eggs, oil and milk, beat until well combined; cover, stand 30 minutes.

Pour 2 to 3 tablespoons of batter into heated, greased heavy-based crepe pan; cook until browned underneath. Turn crepe, brown other side. Repeat with remaining batter, stirring batter occasionally. You will need 12 crepes for this recipe.

Spread 2 level teaspoons of filling onto each crepe, leaving 2cm border. Brush edges with extra egg, fold in sides, roll up to enclose filling. Secure with toothpicks.

Just before serving, deep-fry rolls in hot extra oil until browned; drain on absorbent paper; remove toothpicks. Serve sesame onion rolls with honey plum sauce.

Onion Filling: Heat butter and oil in pan, add onions, garlic and sugar, cover, cook over low heat about 45 minutes or until lightly browned, stirring occasionally. Stir in flour, sauce and chives, stir until mixture boils and thickens; cool.

Honey Plum Sauce: Combine plum sauce and sherry in pan, simmer, uncovered, until reduced to about ½ cup. Stir in honey and soy sauce.

- Sesame onion rolls and honey plum sauce can be prepared a day ahead.
- Storage: Covered, in refrigerator.
- Freeze: Not suitable.
- Microwave: Honey plum sauce suitable.

PRAWN AND LEMON GRASS SALAD

900g uncooked medium prawns
½ radicchio lettuce
½ green oak leaf lettuce
⅓ cup (about 55g) snow pea sprouts
2 tablespoons chopped fresh
   coriander

MARINADE
½ cup lime juice
½ teaspoon sesame oil
1 teaspoon fish sauce
1 tablespoon light soy sauce
3 cloves garlic, crushed
1 teaspoon chopped small fresh
   green chillies
1 tablespoon chopped fresh
   lemon grass
2 tablespoons chopped fresh mint

DRESSING
2 tablespoons lime juice
1 teaspoon grated fresh ginger
3 cloves garlic, crushed
1 tablespoon chopped fresh
   lemon grass
1 tablespoon chopped fresh basil
1 tablespoon chopped fresh
   coriander
⅔ cup coconut cream

Shell and devein prawns, leaving tails intact. Combine prawns and marinade in bowl, cover, refrigerate several hours or overnight.

Just before serving, drain prawns from marinade, discard marinade. Grill or barbecue prawns until tender. Arrange torn lettuce leaves and sprouts on plates, top with warm prawns, drizzle with dressing and sprinkle with coriander.

Marinade: Combine all ingredients in bowl; mix well.

Dressing: Blend or process all ingredients until smooth.

- ■ Prawns can be marinated a day ahead.
- ■ Storage: Covered, in refrigerator.
- ■ Freeze: Not suitable.
- ■ Microwave: Not suitable.

LEFT: Sesame Onion Rolls with Honey Plum Sauce.
ABOVE: Prawn and Lemon Grass Salad.

CITRUS DUCK WITH SPICY GINGER GLAZE

6 duck breast fillets
1 tablespoon oil
1 cup dry white wine
1 tablespoon green ginger wine
2 tablespoons honey
½ cup chicken stock
1 tablespoon light soy sauce
¼ teaspoon sambal oelek

MARINADE
2 tablespoons grated orange rind
1 cup orange juice
2 tablespoons grated fresh ginger
¼ cup honey
½ cup green ginger wine

Trim excess fat from duck. Combine duck and marinade in bowl, cover, refrigerate several hours or overnight.

Remove duck from marinade, reserve marinade. Heat oil in pan, add duck in single layer, skin side down, cook until well browned, turn and brown other side; transfer duck to baking dish in single layer.

Just before serving, bake duck, uncovered, in hot oven about 15 minutes or until tender.

Meanwhile, to complete glaze, combine reserved marinade, white wine and ginger wine in pan, simmer, uncovered, until liquid is reduced by half. Stir in remaining ingredients, simmer, uncovered, until glaze thickens slightly; strain. Serve duck sliced on saute bok choy with noodles and glaze.

Marinade: Combine all ingredients in bowl; mix well.

- ■ Duck can be marinated a day ahead.
- ■ Storage: Covered, in refrigerator.
- ■ Freeze: Not suitable.
- ■ Microwave: Not suitable.

SAUTE BOK CHOY WITH NOODLES

250g thick egg noodles
1 tablespoon oil
2 cloves garlic, crushed
7 green shallots, chopped
2 bunches (about 850g) baby bok choy, shredded
2 sticks celery, chopped
1 tablespoon hoi sin sauce

Add noodles to pan of boiling water, boil, uncovered, about 3 minutes or until tender; drain.

Just before serving, heat oil in pan or wok, add garlic, cook, stirring, 1 minute. Add shallots, bok choy and celery, cook, stirring, until bok choy is just wilted. Add noodles and sauce, cook, stirring, until heated through.

- ■ Recipe best made close to serving.
- ■ Freeze: Not suitable.
- ■ Microwave: Noodles suitable.

BLUEBERRY MANGO TARTLETS WITH STRAWBERRY SAUCE

1½ cups plain flour
125g butter
2 egg yolks
2 tablespoons water, approximately
400g blueberries
2 medium (about 860g) mangoes

FILLING
250g packet cream cheese, softened
1 medium (about 430g) mango, chopped
⅓ cup icing sugar
2 tablespoons lemon juice

STRAWBERRY SAUCE
250g strawberries
1½ tablespoons icing sugar
1 teaspoon Grand Marnier

Grease 6 deep 10cm flan tins. Sift flour into bowl, rub in butter. Add egg yolks and enough water to make ingredients cling together. Press dough into ball, knead gently on lightly floured surface until smooth, cover, refrigerate 30 minutes.

Divide pastry into 6 portions, roll on floured surface until large enough to line prepared tins. Lift pastry into tins, ease into sides, trim edges. Place tins on oven tray, line pastry with paper, fill with dried beans or rice. Bake in moderately hot oven 10 minutes, remove paper and beans, bake 10 minutes or until lightly browned; cool.

Just before serving, pour filling into pastry cases, top with blueberries. Serve with strawberry sauce and sliced mangoes.

Filling: Blend or process all ingredients until smooth.
Strawberry Sauce: Blend or process all ingredients until smooth; strain.

- ■ Pastry cases, filling and sauce can be made a day ahead.
- ■ Storage: Pastry cases, in airtight container. Filling and sauce, covered, in refrigerator.
- ■ Freeze: Pastry cases suitable.
- ■ Microwave: Not suitable.

LEFT: Citrus Duck with Spicy Ginger Glaze served on Saute Bok Choy with Noodles.
ABOVE: Blueberry Mango Tartlets with Strawberry Sauce.

China, black tray, coaster, chopsticks and holder from Made in Japan Imports; tablecloth, black and white mat, serviette and ring from Accoutrement.

Good Value Vegetarian

Serves 6

Carrot and Red Pepper Soup
chardonnay

❦

Minted Ratatouille Lasagne
Snow Pea Salad with Mustard Dressing
chardonnay

❦

Grape and Citrus Compote with Cointreau Cream
chardonnay

❦

Fresh and pretty food like this is surprisingly low cost, and a
healthy treat for anyone, vegetarian or not. Just before serving,
make the easy cheesy pita triangles to go with soup that needs only
reheating. The lasagne needs only reheating, too, before serving
with prepared salad and dressing. Refreshingly, at the last, our
compote of citrus fruit and grapes is lovely with Cointreau cream;
the compote can be made ahead, but the Cointreau cream is best
made just before serving.

CARROT AND RED PEPPER SOUP

7 medium (about 1.4kg) red peppers
2 tablespoons oil
3 medium (about 450g) onions,
    finely chopped
3 cloves garlic, crushed
2 tablespoons grated fresh ginger
1 teaspoon cumin seeds
5 medium (about 600g) carrots,
    chopped
2 teaspoons sugar
1 cup dry white wine
425g can tomato puree
1½ cups water
300ml carton cream

CHEESY PITA TRIANGLES
2 pita breads
⅓ cup grated mozzarella cheese
⅓ cup grated parmesan cheese
10g butter, melted

Quarter peppers, remove seeds and membranes, place peppers on oven tray. Grill peppers, skin side up, until skin blisters and blackens. Peel away skin.

Heat oil in pan, add onions, garlic, ginger and seeds, cook, stirring, until onions are soft. Add peppers and carrots, cook, stirring, until carrots start to soften. Stir in sugar, wine, puree and water, simmer, uncovered, until carrots are tender. Blend or process soup in batches until smooth. Strain soup, return to pan, add cream, stir over heat, without boiling, until hot. Serve carrot and red pepper soup topped with cheesy pita triangles.

Cheesy Pita Triangles: Cut pita breads in half, cut each half into 4 triangles, place triangles on oven tray. Split triangles, fill with combined cheeses, brush with butter, grill until lightly browned all over.

- Carrot and red pepper soup can be made a day ahead. Cheesy pita triangles best made close to serving.
- Storage: Soup, covered, in refrigerator.
- Freeze: Soup suitable.
- Microwave: Not suitable.

MINTED RATATOUILLE LASAGNE

1 bunch (about 650g) English
    spinach, shredded
60g butter
½ cup plain flour
2 cloves garlic, crushed
3 cups milk
8 sheets instant lasagne pasta
2 tablespoons stale breadcrumbs

RATATOUILLE
1 medium (about 400g) eggplant,
    chopped
coarse cooking salt
1 tablespoon oil
2 medium (about 300g) onions,
    chopped
2 tablespoons plain flour
400g mushrooms, sliced
1 medium (about 200g) green pepper,
    chopped
2 x 410g cans tomatoes
2 tablespoons tomato paste
2 tablespoons chopped fresh mint
2 teaspoons sugar

Boil, steam or microwave spinach until just wilted, rinse under cold water; drain. Squeeze excess liquid from spinach; chop finely. Heat butter in pan, add flour and garlic, cook, stirring until mixture is dry and grainy. Gradually stir in milk, stir over heat until mixture boils and thickens. Stir in spinach.

Spread one-third of ratatouille mixture over base of ovenproof dish (8 cup capacity). Top with 4 sheets of pasta, then half the remaining ratatouille and remaining pasta. Spread with remaining ratatouille, then spinach sauce; sprinkle with breadcrumbs. Bake, uncovered, in moderately hot oven about 30 minutes or until pasta is tender.

Ratatouille: Sprinkle eggplant with salt, stand 30 minutes, rinse under cold water; drain, pat dry with absorbent paper.

Heat oil in pan, add onions, cook, stirring, until onions are soft. Add flour, cook, stirring, until mixture is dry and grainy. Add eggplant, mushrooms, pepper, undrained crushed tomatoes and paste, stir over heat until mixture boils and thickens. Simmer, uncovered, until mixture is thick and vegetables soft. Stir in mint and sugar.

- Recipe can be made a day ahead.
- Storage: Covered, in refrigerator.
- Freeze: Not suitable.
- Microwave: Sauce suitable.

SNOW PEA SALAD WITH MUSTARD DRESSING

150g snow peas
1 butter lettuce
1 cos lettuce
3 small (about 195g) zucchini, chopped
1 small (about 170g) green cucumber, chopped

MUSTARD DRESSING
3 teaspoons seeded mustard
½ cup olive oil
¼ cup lemon juice
½ teaspoon sugar

Boil, steam or microwave peas until tender, drain. Rinse under cold water, drain. Tear lettuce into pieces. Combine peas, lettuce, zucchini and cucumber in bowl, toss with mustard dressing.

Mustard Dressing: Combine all ingredients in jar; shake well.

- Snow pea salad can be prepared 3 hours ahead. Mustard dressing can be made a day ahead.
- Storage: Covered, in refrigerator.
- Freeze: Not suitable.
- Microwave: Snow peas suitable.

LEFT: Carrot and Red Pepper Soup.
RIGHT: Minted Ratatouille Lasagne with Snow Pea Salad with Mustard Dressing.

GRAPE AND CITRUS COMPOTE WITH COINTREAU CREAM

2 medium (about 160g) limes
5 medium (about 1.5kg) grapefruit
5 medium (about 850g) oranges
¾ cup grapefruit juice
¼ cup lime juice
½ cup orange juice
½ cup sugar
700g seedless white grapes
700g black grapes
2 tablespoons Cointreau

COINTREAU CREAM
300ml carton thickened cream
1 tablespoon icing sugar
2 tablespoons Cointreau

Peel rind thinly from limes, 1 grapefruit and 1 orange with vegetable peeler, cut rind into thin strips. Peel remaining grapefruit and oranges, remove any white pith from all grapefruit and oranges, cut between membranes into segments.

To make syrup, combine juices and sugar in pan, stir over heat, without boiling, until sugar is dissolved. Add rind strips, boil 2 minutes, without stirring.

Place grapes in large bowl, pour hot syrup over grapes; cool. Remove grapes from syrup, reserve grapes. Bring syrup to boil in pan, simmer, uncovered, until syrup is reduced by half and thickened; stir in liqueur. Pour mixture over grapes; cool. Stir in citrus segments. Serve grape and

citrus compote topped with Cointreau cream.
Cointreau Cream: Beat cream and sifted icing sugar in small bowl until firm, fold in liqueur.

■ Grape and citrus compote can be made a day ahead. Cointreau cream best made close to serving.
■ Storage: Covered, in refrigerator.
■ Freeze: Not suitable.
■ Microwave: Not suitable.

ABOVE: Grape and Citrus Compote with Cointreau Cream.

Table accessories from Country Road Homewares except for stemmed glass dessert dish, from Waterford Wedgwood.

Time for Romance

Serves 2

Campari Cocktails

Gazpacho with Avocado in Crouton Baskets

medium-dry chenin blanc

Chicken Medallions with Mushroom Thyme Sauce

Crisp Leek Curls

Buttery Wine Risotto

chardonnay or chenin blanc

Coconut Mousses with Golden Fruit Salad

light sweet white

Any day with special meaning for just the two of you is a reason to celebrate with soft lights, sweet music and our fabulous dinner. Start with sparkling cocktails, then continue with sparkling wine, if you like, or follow our wine suggestions. Start preparations the day before, so you'll have only minor details to complete. Just before serving, chop the avocado, stir into gazpacho and assemble crouton baskets. Allow about 20 minutes to bake the chicken, make sauce, deep-fry leek curls and finish the risotto. About 2 hours before that, turn mousses onto meringue bases, ready to serve with fresh fruit salad.

CAMPARI COCKTAILS

2 tablespoons Campari
375ml bottle dry sparkling wine,
chilled

Just before serving, pour Campari into chilled glasses, top with dry sparkling wine.

■ Must be made just before serving.

GAZPACHO WITH AVOCADO IN CROUTON BASKETS

We used egg tomatoes in this recipe; any full-flavoured tomatoes can be used.

1 tablespoon olive oil
1 medium (about 150g) onion,
chopped
2 cloves garlic, crushed
3 medium (about 150g) egg
tomatoes, chopped
½ cup chicken stock
½ teaspoon sugar
dash tabasco sauce
4 cooked king prawns
1 medium egg tomato, seeded, extra
½ small green cucumber, seeded
¼ medium avocado
1 green shallot, sliced

CROUTON BASKETS
⅓ loaf unsliced white bread
oil for deep-frying

Heat oil in pan, add onion and garlic, cook, stirring, until onion is soft. Add tomatoes, stock and sugar, simmer, covered, about 25 minutes or until tomatoes are pulpy. Push tomato mixture through sieve, discard pulp. Stir in sauce, cover, refrigerate until cold.

Shell and devein prawns, leaving heads and tails intact. Finely chop extra tomato and cucumber.

Just before serving, finely chop avocado, stir into chilled tomato mixture with extra tomato, cucumber and shallot. Spoon gazpacho into crouton baskets, serve with prawns.

Crouton Baskets: Remove crusts from bread, cut bread into 2 x 4cm slices. Hollow out centre from each slice, leaving bases intact to form square basket shapes. Deep-fry in hot oil until lightly browned and crisp; drain on absorbent paper; cool.

■ Recipe can be prepared a day ahead.
■ Storage: Tomato mixture, covered, in refrigerator. Baskets, in airtight container.
■ Freeze: Uncooked unfilled baskets suitable.
■ Microwave: Tomato mixture suitable.

CHICKEN MEDALLIONS WITH MUSHROOM THYME SAUCE

2 chicken breast fillets
20g butter
4 green shallots, chopped
1 clove garlic, crushed
1 bacon rasher, chopped
1 large (about 50g) flat mushroom,
chopped
½ medium red pepper, finely
chopped
1 tablespoon chopped fresh
flat-leafed parsley
½ teaspoon chopped fresh thyme
½ teaspoon chicken stock powder
plain flour
1 tablespoon oil
1 tablespoon oil, extra

MUSHROOM THYME SAUCE
2 teaspoons oil
½ teaspoon chicken stock powder
½ cup dry white wine
½ cup cream
1 teaspoon chopped fresh thyme
¼ teaspoon cornflour
1 teaspoon water

Carefully remove tenderloin from chicken breasts, as shown. Remove white sinew from tenderloins, process tenderloins until finely minced, transfer to bowl.

Heat butter in pan, add shallots and garlic, cook, stirring, until shallots are soft. Add bacon, mushroom and pepper, cook, stirring, until bacon is lightly browned and mushroom is soft; cool. Reserve 2 tablespoons of shallot mixture for sauce. Add remaining shallot mixture, parsley, thyme and stock powder to minced chicken; mix well.

Cut a pocket in 1 side of each chicken breast, taking care not to cut right through. Carefully push mince mixture into pockets; secure openings with toothpicks.

Toss chicken in flour, shake away excess flour. Heat oil in pan, add chicken, cook until browned. Transfer chicken to baking dish, sprinkle with extra oil.

Just before serving, bake chicken, uncovered, in moderately hot oven about 20 minutes or until chicken is tender. Serve chicken sliced with mushroom thyme sauce. Serve with crisp leek curls and buttery wine risotto.

Mushroom Thyme Sauce: Heat oil in pan, add reserved shallot mixture, cook, stirring, 1 minute. Add stock powder and wine, simmer, uncovered, until mixture is reduced by half.

Just before serving, stir in cream, thyme and blended cornflour and water, stir over heat until sauce boils and thickens slightly.

- Recipe can prepared a day ahead.
- Storage: Covered, in refrigerator.
- Freeze: Not suitable.
- Microwave: Not suitable.

CRISP LEEK CURLS

½ medium leek
oil for deep-frying

Cut halfway through length of leek, separate leaves and lay flat (you will need 4 leaves for this recipe, reserve remaining leek for another use). Cut leaves diagonally into 1cm strips. Place in bowl, cover with water, refrigerate 2 hours. Drain strips; pat dry with absorbent paper.

Just before serving, deep-fry leek strips in batches in hot oil until browned and crisp; drain on absorbent paper.

- Recipe best prepared 2 hours ahead.
- Storage: Covered, in refrigerator.
- Freeze: Not suitable.
- Microwave: Not suitable.

BUTTERY WINE RISOTTO

20g butter
½ medium onion, finely chopped
1 clove garlic, crushed
¾ cup arborio rice
pinch turmeric
2 tablespoons dry white wine
2 cups chicken stock
20g butter, extra
2 tablespoons grated parmesan
cheese

Heat butter in pan, add onion and garlic, cook, stirring, until onion is soft. Add rice and turmeric, stir until rice is well coated. Add wine and ¼ cup of stock. Simmer, stirring, until liquid is absorbed. Add remaining stock in about 4 batches, stirring until liquid is absorbed before adding more stock. Total cooking time should be about 20 minutes or until rice is tender.

Just before serving, stir in extra butter and cheese.

- Recipe best made just before serving.
- Freeze: Not suitable.
- Microwave: Not suitable.

LEFT: Gazpacho with Avocado in Crouton Baskets.
ABOVE: Chicken Medallions with Mushroom Thyme Sauce, Crisp Leek Curls and Buttery Wine Risotto.

Lightly oil 2 moulds (⅔ cup capacity). Sprinkle gelatine over water in cup, stand in pan of simmering water, stir until dissolved; cool slightly. Beat egg yolks and sugar in small bowl with electric mixer until thick and creamy, stir in coconut cream, liqueur and gelatine mixture.

Beat thickened cream and essence in small bowl until soft peaks form, fold into coconut cream mixture. Pour into prepared moulds, refrigerate until set. Turn mousses onto meringues, refrigerate 2 hours.

Just before serving, top mousses with coconut and chocolate palm trees, serve with golden fruit salad.

Meringues: Grease an oven tray, cover with baking paper. Trace around base of coconut mousse moulds to give 2 circles on paper.

Beat egg whites in small bowl with electric mixer until soft peaks form, gradually add sugar, beat until dissolved between additions. Spoon meringue mixture into piping bag fitted with 1cm plain tube, pipe mixture over circles marked on paper. Bake meringues in very slow oven for about 1 hour or until firm to touch. Turn oven off, cool meringues in oven with door ajar. When meringues are cold, carefully remove from trays.

Golden Fruit Salad: Cut fruit into 1cm cubes, combine in bowl.

Chocolate Palm Trees: Place chocolate into piping bag fitted with fine plain tube, pipe palm tree shapes onto baking paper or foil; copy palm trees from our picture. Leave at room temperature to set.

- ■ Recipe can be prepared a day ahead.
- ■ Storage: Mousses and golden fruit salad, covered, in refrigerator. Meringues, in airtight container. Chocolate palm trees, at room temperature.
- ■ Freeze: Not suitable.
- ■ Microwave: Gelatine suitable.

COCONUT MOUSSES WITH GOLDEN FRUIT SALAD

2 teaspoons gelatine
1 tablespoon water
2 egg yolks
⅓ cup castor sugar
½ cup coconut cream
1 tablespoon Malibu
½ cup thickened cream
¼ teaspoon coconut essence
2 tablespoons shredded coconut, toasted

MERINGUES
1 egg white
¼ cup castor sugar

GOLDEN FRUIT SALAD
½ medium mango
1 medium (about 90g) kiwi fruit
½ small (about 500g) rockmelon
2 tablespoons passionfruit pulp

CHOCOLATE PALM TREES
50g Choc Melts, melted

LEFT: Coconut Mousses with Golden Fruit Salad.

China from Wedgwood.

New Year's Eve Party

Serves 10

Oyster and Pine Nut Triangles

sparkling white wine

Eggplant Sandwiches with Tomato Vinaigrette

dry semillon or chablis

Barbecued Butterflied Lamb with Polenta

Green Salad with Peaches and Snow Pea Sprouts

Beetroot and Red Cabbage Salad

light red wine or beaujolais

Passionfruit Sorbet with Kiwi Fruit Mint Sauce

Coconut Shortbread

light spatlese riesling

A gala night of fun and high spirits demands a sensational dinner, and it can be relaxing for
you, too, because so much is done ahead. Just before serving, the pastries are baked,
the colourful "sandwich" layers are assembled, the marinated lamb is barbecued,
the polenta is reheated and the green salad tossed; the red salad is completely prepared.
Then the move to dessert is easy with icy passionfruit sorbet in the freezer,
ready to serve with a quick sauce and already-made coconut shortbread.

OYSTER AND PINE NUT TRIANGLES

4 x 105g cans smoked oysters, drained, chopped
⅔ cup pine nuts, toasted
1 cup (70g) stale breadcrumbs
1½ teaspoons grated lemon rind
⅓ cup lemon juice
18 sheets fillo pastry
150g butter, melted

Combine oysters, pine nuts, breadcrumbs, rind and juice in bowl. Layer 2 sheets of pastry together, brushing each with a little butter. Cut layered sheets into 4 strips lengthways. Place 2 level teaspoons of oyster mixture on narrow end of 1 strip. Fold 1 corner end of pastry diagonally across to other edge to form a triangle. Continue folding to end of strip, retaining triangular shape. Brush triangle with a little more butter, place on greased oven tray. Repeat with remaining pastry, butter and oyster mixture.

Just before serving, bake triangles in moderately hot oven about 20 minutes or until browned and crisp.

Makes 36.

■ Recipe can be prepared a day ahead.
■ Storage: Covered, in refrigerator.
■ Freeze: Uncooked triangles suitable.
■ Microwave: Not suitable.

BELOW: Oyster and Pine Nut Triangles.
RIGHT: Eggplant Sandwiches with Tomato Vinaigrette.

EGGPLANT SANDWICHES WITH TOMATO VINAIGRETTE

We used egg tomatoes in this recipe; any full-flavoured tomatoes can be used.

2 medium (about 600g) eggplants
oil for deep-frying
2 large (about 400g) red peppers
400g piece goats' cheese

PESTO
2 cups firmly packed fresh
**   basil leaves**
½ cup olive oil
1 clove garlic, crushed
⅔ cup grated parmesan cheese

TOMATO VINAIGRETTE
2 medium (about 100g) egg
**   tomatoes, chopped**
⅔ cup olive oil
2 tablespoons white vinegar
½ teaspoon sugar

Cut each eggplant into 10 slices about 1cm thick. Deep-fry eggplant in hot oil until browned, drain on absorbent paper; cool.

Quarter peppers, remove seeds and membranes. Grill peppers, skin side up, until skin blisters and blackens. Peel away skin, cut peppers into 2cm strips; cool.

Using hot knife, cut cheese into 10 slices about 8mm thick.

Just before serving, place an eggplant slice on serving plate, top with a slice of cheese, 2 strips of pepper, pesto, another slice of eggplant and some more pesto. Spoon tomato vinaigrette onto plate. Repeat with remaining ingredients.

Pesto: Blend basil, oil and garlic until smooth; stir in cheese.

Tomato Vinaigrette: Blend tomatoes until smooth, push through sieve; discard pulp. Combine tomato puree with remaining ingredients in jar; shake well.

- Eggplants, pesto, cheese and vinaigrette can be prepared several hours ahead.
- Storage: Separately, covered, in refrigerator.
- Freeze: Not suitable.
- Microwave: Not suitable.

69

BARBECUED BUTTERFLIED LAMB WITH POLENTA

2 x 1.75kg legs of lamb, butterflied

MARINADE
1 medium lemon
½ cup lemon juice
¾ cup olive oil
2 tablespoons cracked black pepper
10 cloves garlic, crushed
2 teaspoons Dijon mustard
**2 tablespoons chopped fresh
   rosemary**

POLENTA
1 litre (4 cups) chicken stock
1 cup (200g) polenta
½ cup grated parmesan cheese
2 egg yolks
plain flour
oil for deep-frying

Place lamb in marinade, cover, refrigerate overnight.

Remove lamb from marinade; discard marinade. Barbecue lamb over low heat until tender, or bake, uncovered, in moderately hot oven about 20 minutes or until cooked as desired. Serve lamb sliced with polenta. Serve with salads.

Marinade: Remove rind from lemon, using vegetable peeler; cut rind into thin strips. Combine rind with remaining ingredients in large bowl.

Polenta: Grease 20cm x 30cm lamington pan. Bring stock to boil, gradually add polenta, simmer, uncovered, about 15 minutes or until thick, stirring occasionally. Cool mixture 1 minute, stir in cheese and egg yolks. Spread mixture into prepared pan, cool, cover, refrigerate until cold.

Cut polenta into triangles, toss in flour,

shake away excess flour. Deep-fry triangles in hot oil until browned; drain on absorbent paper.

Just before serving, place triangles on hot griddle or in hot pan, cook until triangles are heated through.

- ■ Recipe can be prepared a day ahead.
- ■ Storage: Covered, in refrigerator.
- ■ Freeze: Not suitable.
- ■ Microwave: Not suitable.

GREEN SALAD WITH PEACHES AND SNOW PEA SPROUTS

1 butter lettuce
1 cos lettuce
1 red oak leaf lettuce
3 medium (about 750g) avocados, sliced
3 medium (about 600g) peaches, sliced
160g snow pea sprouts

DRESSING
½ cup olive oil
¼ cup oil
¼ cup balsamic vinegar
2 tablespoons chopped fresh chives

Combine torn lettuce leaves, avocados, peaches and sprouts in large bowl. Add dressing, toss lightly.
Dressing: Combine all ingredients in jar; shake well.

- ■ Dressing can be made a day ahead.
- ■ Storage: Covered, in refrigerator.
- ■ Freeze: Not suitable.

BEETROOT AND RED CABBAGE SALAD

250g sugar snap peas
4 medium (about 650g) beetroot, coarsely grated
½ medium (about 750g) red cabbage, finely shredded

DRESSING
2 teaspoons grated orange rind
⅓ cup orange juice
½ cup oil
2 tablespoons cider vinegar
1 tablespoon poppy seeds

Add peas to pan of boiling water, boil 1 minute, drain. Rinse under cold water, drain well. Combine peas, beetroot and cabbage in bowl, add dressing; toss well.
Dressing: Combine all ingredients in jar; shake well.

- ■ Recipe can be prepared several hours ahead.
- ■ Storage: Covered, in refrigerator.
- ■ Freeze: Not suitable.
- ■ Microwave: Peas suitable.

LEFT: Barbecued Butterflied Lamb with Polenta and Beetroot and Red Cabbage Salad.
ABOVE: Green Salad with Peaches and Snow Pea Sprouts.

PASSIONFRUIT SORBET WITH KIWI FRUIT MINT SAUCE

1⅓ cups castor sugar
2½ cups water
24 passionfruit
4 egg whites

KIWI FRUIT MINT SAUCE
20 medium (about 1.8kg) kiwi fruit
⅔ cup sparkling mineral water
2 tablespoons chopped fresh mint
1 tablespoon castor sugar

Combine sugar and water in pan. Stir over heat, without boiling, until sugar is dissolved. Simmer, uncovered, about 12 minutes, without stirring, or until mixture begins to thicken slightly; cool. Remove pulp from passionfruit (you need 2 cups of pulp for this recipe). Stir pulp into sugar syrup, pour into lamington pan; cover, freeze until just firm.

Remove mixture from pan, beat with electric mixer in bowl until thick and fluffy. Return mixture to pan, cover, freeze until just firm.

Repeat beating process, add egg whites 1 at a time, beat until fluffy. Transfer mixture to 15cm x 25cm loaf pan, cover, freeze until firm. Serve passionfruit sorbet with kiwi fruit mint sauce and coconut shortbread.

Kiwi Fruit Mint Sauce: Blend or process kiwi fruit and 2 tablespoons of the mineral water about 3 seconds or until just combined. Sieve pulp into bowl, discard seeds. Stir in remaining water, mint and sugar, stir until sugar is dissolved.

- Passionfruit sorbet can be made 3 days ahead; kiwi fruit mint sauce best made just before serving.
- Storage: Covered, in freezer.
- Freeze: Sorbet essential; sauce not suitable.
- Microwave: Not suitable.

COCONUT SHORTBREAD

250g butter
¼ teaspoon coconut essence
⅓ cup castor sugar
2¼ cups plain flour
¼ cup rice flour
½ cup coconut

Have butter at room temperature. Beat butter, essence and sugar in small bowl with electric mixer until light and fluffy. Transfer mixture to large bowl, stir in sifted flours and coconut in 2 batches. Turn dough onto floured surface, knead lightly until smooth.

Roll dough between sheets of greaseproof paper until 6mm thick. Cut shapes from dough, place about 3cm apart on lightly greased oven trays. Bake in moderately slow oven about 20 minutes or until lightly browned. Stand few minutes before transferring shortbread to wire rack to cool.

Makes about 40.

- Recipe can be made a week ahead.
- Storage: Airtight container.
- Freeze: Suitable.
- Microwave: Not suitable.

LEFT: Passionfruit Sorbet with Kiwi Fruit Mint Sauce and Coconut Shortbread.

China and glasses from Villeroy & Boch; table and bread basket from Corso de Fiori; plants from Floravin Nursery.

A Taste of Italy

Serves 4

Baby Octopus on Polenta with Red Peppers

verdelho or marsanne

Veal Ragout in Eggplant Charlotte

Tomato Bocconcini Salad

cabernet merlot or chianti style

Hot Apple Souffles with Stewed Rhubarb

spicy gewurztraminer

Italians are renowned for their hospitality, with hearty servings of robust, well-flavoured food such as you can taste here. You can prepare the octopus, make the polenta and charlotte ahead. Just before serving, cook the octopus in rich wine sauce, deep-fry the polenta, cook the red peppers, reheat the charlotte, make the spinach sauce and the quick salad. As a light finish, delicate apple souffles must go hot to the table, although the apple puree and rhubarb can be made ahead.

BABY OCTOPUS ON POLENTA WITH RED PEPPERS

1kg baby octopus
1 tablespoon olive oil
1 medium (about 150g) onion, chopped
3 cloves garlic, crushed
½ cup dry red wine
1 cup tomato puree
¾ cup water
1 tablespoon lime juice
1 tablespoon chopped fresh oregano
3 teaspoons sugar
1 tablespoon chopped fresh parsley

POLENTA
2 cups chicken stock
½ cup polenta
¼ cup grated parmesan cheese
1 egg yolk
oil for deep-frying

RED PEPPERS
2 small (about 300g) red peppers
2 teaspoons olive oil

Remove and discard heads and beaks from octopus. Heat oil in pan, add octopus, onion and garlic, cook, stirring, until octopus change colour. Add wine, puree, water, juice, oregano and sugar, simmer, uncovered, about 1 hour or until octopus are tender. Stir in parsley. Serve octopus on polenta with red peppers.

Polenta: Grease 8cm x 26cm bar pan. Bring stock to boil in saucepan, add polenta, simmer, uncovered, about 15 minutes or until polenta is soft, stirring occasionally. Cool 1 minute. Stir in cheese and egg yolk. Press mixture into prepared pan, cover, refrigerate until cold. Turn polenta out, cut into 4 pieces. Deep-fry polenta in hot oil until lightly browned; drain on absorbent paper.

Red Peppers: Quarter peppers, remove seeds and membranes. Grill peppers, skin side up, until skin blisters and blackens. Cool peppers, peel away skins, cut peppers into thin strips. Toss peppers in oil.

- Octopus can be prepared a day ahead. Deep-fry polenta just before serving. Red peppers best made just before serving.
- Storage: Covered, in refrigerator.
- Freeze: Not suitable.
- Microwave: Not suitable.

VEAL RAGOUT IN EGGPLANT CHARLOTTE

2 tablespoons stale breadcrumbs
3 medium (about 1kg) eggplants
½ cup olive oil

FILLING
1kg shoulder of veal, boned
2 tablespoons olive oil
200g baby mushrooms, quartered
1 medium (about 150g) onion, chopped
2 cloves garlic, crushed
2 large (about 400g) potatoes, chopped
1 tablespoon olive oil, extra
¼ cup tomato paste
410g can tomatoes
⅔ cup dry red wine
1½ cups beef stock
1 bay leaf
1 teaspoon sugar
1 cup (70g) stale breadcrumbs
2 eggs, lightly beaten

SPINACH SAUCE
1 tablespoon olive oil
1 clove garlic, crushed
¾ bunch (about 500g) English
spinach, shredded
¾ cup chicken stock
1 teaspoon sugar
⅓ cup cream
1 teaspoon cornflour
2 teaspoons water

Line deep 23cm round cake pan with foil, grease foil, sprinkle base and side with breadcrumbs. Cut eggplants into 1cm slices, brush slices with oil, place eggplant slices in single layer on oven trays, grill both sides until lightly browned.

Arrange overlapping slices on base and side of prepared pan, reserving enough slices to cover filling. Spoon filling over eggplant, press down firmly. Top with remaining eggplant slices, press firmly, cover with foil, bake in moderate oven about 45 minutes or until heated through. Stand 5 minutes before turning out; serve with spinach sauce. Serve with tomato bocconcini salad.

Filling: Cut veal into thin strips. Heat half the oil in large pan, add mushrooms, cook until lightly browned, remove from pan; drain on absorbent paper.

Heat remaining oil in same pan, add onion, garlic and potatoes, cook, stirring, until onion is soft. Remove onion mixture from pan; drain on absorbent paper.

Heat extra oil in same pan, add veal in batches, cook, stirring, until well browned. Add tomato paste, undrained crushed tomatoes, wine, stock, bay leaf and sugar, cover, simmer 15 minutes. Stir in mushrooms and onion mixture, simmer, uncovered, 15 minutes or until mixture thickens and most of the liquid has evaporated. Cool 5 minutes, discard bay leaf, stir in breadcrumbs and eggs.

Spinach Sauce: Heat oil in pan, add garlic and spinach, cook 1 minute or until spinach is wilted. Add stock, simmer, covered, 5 minutes or until spinach is very soft. Blend or process spinach mixture until smooth. Return to pan, stir in sugar, cream and blended cornflour and water, stir constantly over heat until mixture boils and thickens slightly.

- Eggplant charlotte can be made a day ahead. Spinach sauce best made just before serving.
- Storage: Covered, in refrigerator.
- Freeze: Not suitable.
- Microwave: Not suitable.

TOMATO BOCCONCINI SALAD

We used egg tomatoes in this recipe; any full-flavoured tomatoes can be used.

3 large (about 225g) egg
tomatoes, sliced
150g bocconcini, sliced
1 medium (about 170g) red Spanish
onion, sliced

DRESSING
⅓ cup olive oil
1 tablespoon balsamic vinegar
1 clove garlic, crushed
2 tablespoons shredded fresh basil

Layer tomatoes, cheese and onion on serving platter. Pour dressing over salad.
Dressing: Combine all ingredients in jar; shake well.

- Recipe best made just before serving.
- Freeze: Not suitable.

BELOW LEFT: Baby Octopus on Polenta with Red Peppers.
BELOW: Veal Ragout in Eggplant Charlotte with Tomato Bocconcini Salad.

HOT APPLE SOUFFLES WITH STEWED RHUBARB

½ small (about 80g) apple, finely
   chopped
1 tablespoon Calvados or brandy
½ cup castor sugar
¼ cup water
4 egg whites
2 tablespoons castor sugar, extra

APPLE PUREE
3 large (about 600g) apples, finely
   chopped
⅓ cup water
2 tablespoons Calvados or brandy

STEWED RHUBARB
3 cups (about 500g) chopped
   fresh rhubarb
⅓ cup castor sugar

Lightly grease 4 souffle dishes (1 cup capacity), sprinkle bases and sides with about 1 tablespoon castor sugar, shake away excess sugar. Combine apple and brandy in bowl, cover, stand 30 minutes.

Combine the ½ cup of sugar and water in pan, stir over heat, without boiling, until sugar is dissolved. Boil, uncovered, without stirring, about 4 minutes or until syrup reaches 115°C on a candy thermometer, or when a teaspoon of syrup forms a soft ball when dropped into a cup of cold water. Allow bubbles to subside, combine apple puree and syrup in bowl.

Beat egg whites in small bowl with electric mixer until soft peaks form. Gradually add extra sugar, beat until dissolved. Gently fold egg white mixture into warm apple mixture in 2 batches.

Spoon half the mixture into prepared dishes, sprinkle with apple and brandy mixture, top with remaining souffle mixture; smooth tops with spatula. Place dishes on oven tray, bake in moderately hot oven about 15 minutes or until souffles are well risen and browned. Serve immediately with stewed rhubarb and cream. Dust with icing sugar, if desired.

Apple Puree: Combine apples and water in pan, simmer, covered, about 5 minutes or until apples are soft, drain. Blend or process apples and brandy until smooth.

Stewed Rhubarb: Combine rhubarb and sugar in pan, simmer, uncovered, about 8 minutes or until rhubarb is pulpy, stirring occasionally. Cool to room temperature.

- Souffles must be made just before serving. Rhubarb and apple puree can be cooked a day ahead.
- Storage: Rhubarb and apple puree, separately, covered, in refrigerator.
- Freeze: Not suitable.
- Microwave: Rhubarb and apple puree suitable.

LEFT: Hot Apple Souffles with Stewed Rhubarb.

Brilliant for Busy Days

Serves 8

Quail Eggs and Radishes with Mustard Mayonnaise

full-flavoured chardonnay

Asparagus with Leek, Ginger and Prosciutto

fume blanc or sauvignon blanc

Tomato and Basil Chicken

Spinach Gnocchi

full-flavoured chardonnay

Tiramisu with Chocolate and Vanilla Cremes

chilled sweet sherry

One secret of presenting an excellent meal when you're rushed is to have almost everything made ahead, as we've done here. Our pretty appetiser of crunchy radishes and quail eggs with mustard mayonnaise is a cold one. Next, the asparagus starter is easily reheated, as is the chicken casserole; the spinach gnocchi with crispy crumbs cook in next to no time. To crown your success, we've made tiramisu (or "pick me up"), delectable with mascarpone cheese filling and two sauces, all refrigerated.

QUAIL EGGS AND RADISHES WITH MUSTARD MAYONNAISE

24 quail eggs
1 bunch (about 120g) rocket
16 baby radishes
2 tablespoons fine sea salt
2 tablespoons cracked black
    peppercorns

MUSTARD MAYONNAISE
2 egg yolks
2 cloves garlic, crushed
1 tablespoon lemon juice
¾ cup oil
1 teaspoon grated lemon rind
3 teaspoons Dijon mustard

Place eggs in pan, cover with water, bring to boil, simmer 1 minute, drain. Rinse eggs under cold water until cold; drain eggs, peel carefully.

Arrange rocket, radishes and eggs on serving plate. Serve with mustard mayonnaise, salt and pepper.

Mustard Mayonnaise: Whisk egg yolks, garlic and juice in bowl until smooth. Gradually whisk in oil a drop at a time, whisking constantly until a little over quarter of the oil has been added. Pour in remaining oil in a thin stream, whisking constantly. Stir in rind and mustard.

- Quail eggs and radishes can be prepared a day ahead. Mustard mayonnaise can be made 2 days ahead.
- Storage: Eggs and radishes, covered, in refrigerator. Mayonnaise, covered, in refrigerator.
- Freeze: Not suitable.
- Microwave: Not suitable.

ASPARAGUS WITH LEEK, GINGER AND PROSCIUTTO

1 medium lemon
1 small (about 200g) leek
1 piece (about 40g) fresh ginger
50g butter
1 teaspoon ground ginger
250g sliced prosciutto, thinly sliced
40 (about 800g) fresh asparagus
    spears

BALSAMIC VINAIGRETTE
¼ cup lemon juice
1 tablespoon honey
2½ tablespoons balsamic vinegar
⅓ cup olive oil
2 cloves garlic, crushed

Peel rind from lemon using vegetable peeler, cut rind into thin strips. Cut leek into 6cm lengths, cut lengths into thin strips. Finely slice fresh ginger, cut slices into thin strips.

Heat butter in large pan, add leek, both gingers, rind and prosciutto, cook, stirring, until leek starts to soften; keep warm. Boil, steam or microwave asparagus until just tender; drain.

Place asparagus and leek mixture onto serving plates, drizzle with balsamic vinaigrette.

Balsamic Vinaigrette: Combine all ingredients in jar; shake well.

- Asparagus and leek mixture can be cooked several hours ahead. Balsamic vinaigrette can be made a week ahead.
- Storage: Covered, in refrigerator.
- Freeze: Not suitable.
- Microwave: Asparagus suitable.

TOMATO AND BASIL CHICKEN

60g butter
16 chicken thigh fillets, halved
2 medium (about 300g) onions,
chopped
3 large (about 750g) tomatoes,
peeled, chopped
1 small fresh red chilli, finely chopped
¼ cup tomato paste
2 cups chicken stock
1 teaspoon sugar
¼ cup shredded fresh basil

Heat butter in pan, add chicken, cook until browned on both sides; drain on absorbent paper. Drain fat from pan, leaving 1 tablespoon fat in pan. Add onions to pan, cook, stirring, until onions are soft. Add chicken, tomatoes, chilli, paste and stock, simmer, covered, 10 minutes. Uncover, simmer 10 minutes or until chicken is tender and mixture is slightly thickened. Stir in sugar, sprinkle with basil. Serve with spinach gnochi.

- Recipe can be made a day ahead.
- Storage: Covered, in refrigerator.
- Freeze: Suitable.
- Microwave: Not suitable.

SPINACH GNOCCHI

1 bunch (about 650g) English spinach
½ cup plain flour
2½ cups (500g) ricotta cheese
1 cup (80g) grated fresh
parmesan cheese
2 eggs, lightly beaten
¼ teaspoon ground nutmeg
1½ cups (110g) stale breadcrumbs
plain flour, extra
100g butter, melted
2 cups (200g) packaged breadcrumbs
¾ cup finely grated fresh parmesan
cheese, extra

Boil, steam or microwave spinach until just wilted; rinse under cold water, squeeze excess water from spinach, chop finely.

Combine sifted flour, spinach, cheeses, eggs, nutmeg and stale breadcrumbs in bowl. Toss 2 level teaspoons of mixture into some extra flour, shape into an oval. Repeat with remaining mixture. Add gnocchi to pan of simmering water, simmer, uncovered, 2 minutes, drain; keep warm.

Combine butter, packaged breadcrumbs and extra cheese in pan, cook, stirring, until lightly browned; sprinkle breadcrumb mixture over gnocchi.

- Recipe can be prepared a day ahead.
- Storage: Covered, in refrigerator.
- Freeze: Cooked gnocchi suitable.
- Microwave: Spinach suitable.

FAR LEFT: Quail Eggs and Radishes with Mustard Mayonnaise.
LEFT: Asparagus with Leek, Ginger and Prosciutto.
ABOVE: Tomato and Basil Chicken with Spinach Gnocchi.

TIRAMISU WITH CHOCOLATE AND VANILLA CREMES

5 eggs
¾ cup castor sugar
1 cup self-raising flour
90g butter, melted
1 tablespoon dry instant coffee
1 tablespoon hot water
2 tablespoons drinking chocolate
⅓ cup marsala

FILLING
375g mascarpone cheese
¼ cup icing sugar
2 egg yolks

CHOCOLATE CREME
1 cup milk
25g dark chocolate, chopped
2 egg yolks
2 tablespoons castor sugar

VANILLA CREME
1 cup milk
1 vanilla bean
2 egg yolks
2 tablespoons castor sugar

Grease 25cm x 30cm Swiss roll pan, line base and sides with paper; grease paper. Beat eggs in large bowl with electric mixer until thick and creamy. Beat in sugar a tablespoon at a time, beat until dissolved between additions. Fold in sifted flour, then butter and combined coffee and water. Spread mixture into prepared pan. Bake in moderately hot oven about 15 minutes or until firm to touch.

Turn cake immediately onto baking paper sprinkled with sifted drinking chocolate. Trim edges of cake, roll up in paper from long side, stand 2 minutes, unroll, cool. Brush cake with marsala, spread with filling, roll up, cover, refrigerate several hours or overnight. Serve roll sliced with chocolate and vanilla cremes.

Filling: Beat cheese, sifted icing sugar and yolks in small bowl with electric mixer until light and fluffy.

Chocolate Creme: Combine milk and chocolate in small pan, stir over low heat until chocolate is melted; cool. Beat egg yolks and sugar in small bowl with electric mixer until thick and creamy, gradually add chocolate mixture. Return mixture to pan, stir over low heat, without boiling, about 15 minutes or until mixture is slightly thickened. Strain mixture, cover, cool, refrigerate several hours or overnight.

Vanilla Creme: Combine milk and split vanilla bean in small pan, bring to boil, remove from heat, stand 15 minutes. Strain mixture through cloth. Beat yolks and sugar in small bowl with electric mixer until thick and creamy, gradually add milk. Return mixture to pan, stir over low heat, without boiling, about 15 minutes or until slightly thickened. Strain mixture, cover, cool, refrigerate 3 hours or overnight.

- Tiramisu can be made and filled a day ahead. Chocolate and vanilla cremes can be made a day ahead.
- Storage: Covered, in refrigerator.
- Freeze: Not suitable.
- Microwave: Not suitable.

ABOVE: Tiramisu with Chocolate and Vanilla Cremes.

China from Hale Imports; glasses and place mats from Accoutrement; cutlery from Georg Jensen; vase and salt and pepper server from The Bay Tree; table from Country Form.

Country Comfort

Serves 6

Tangy Tomato Cocktails

Vegetable Tempura with
Spicy Avocado Sauce

light pale rosé

Herbed Rabbit Casserole

Bacon Lentils

Red and Green Salad

cabernet sauvignon, shiraz or zinfandel

Panettone Custard with
Macerated Fruit

asti spumante

There's a warming, country kitchen mood to this menu in which even the tomato cocktails
are warm; they're nicest mixed just before serving. You'd also dip the vegetable morsels in
light batter then, quickly fry them and serve hot with the spicy, coconutty avocado sauce.
However, the casserole and bacon lentils develop flavour if cooked ahead; they can be
reheated and the salad quickly assembled. For dessert, the fruit should be
macerated overnight in sugar and liqueur; it's delectable with a hot, sweet bread custard.

TANGY TOMATO COCKTAILS

2 x 850ml cans tomato juice
2 teaspoons lemon juice
2 teaspoons Worcestershire sauce
1 teaspoon tabasco sauce
1 teaspoon celery salt
¼ teaspoon ground black pepper
1 cup vodka

Combine juices, sauces, salt and pepper in pan, stir over heat until just simmering. Pour 2 tablespoons of vodka into each glass; top with hot juice mixture.

■ Recipe best made just before serving.
■ Freeze: Not suitable.
■ Microwave: Suitable.

VEGETABLE TEMPURA WITH SPICY AVOCADO SAUCE

250g broccoli, chopped
¼ medium (about 250g) cauliflower, chopped
150g snow peas
1 bunch (about 250g) fresh asparagus spears, halved
plain flour
oil for deep-frying

BATTER
3 cups plain flour
3 eggs
2¼ cups cold water

SPICY AVOCADO SAUCE
2 teaspoons oil
1 clove garlic, crushed
1 teaspoon grated fresh ginger
½ teaspoon ground cumin
½ teaspoon ground coriander
½ teaspoon five spice powder
150g can coconut milk
1 medium (about 250g) avocado, chopped
⅓ cup milk

Add broccoli and cauliflower to pan of boiling water, simmer, uncovered, 1 minute, remove broccoli. Simmer cauliflower a further minute, rinse vegetables under cold water; drain. Toss snow peas and asparagus in flour, shake away excess flour. Dip all vegetables into batter. Deep-fry vegetables in hot oil until lightly browned; drain on absorbent paper. Serve vegetable tempura immediately with spicy avocado sauce.

Batter: Sift flour into bowl; gradually beat in combined eggs and water; beat until smooth.

Spicy Avocado Sauce: Heat oil in pan, add garlic, ginger and spices, cook, stirring, until aromatic. Stir in coconut milk. Blend or process coconut milk mixture with avocado and milk until smooth.

■ Recipe best made just before serving.
■ Freeze: Not suitable
■ Microwave: Broccoli and cauliflower suitable.

HERBED RABBIT CASSEROLE

12 (about 1.75kg) rabbit cutlets
plain flour
⅓ cup olive oil
1 medium (about 150g) onion,
**   chopped**
2 cloves garlic, crushed
½ cup dry red wine
1 cup chicken stock
2 x 425g cans tomatoes
2 tablespoons tomato paste
2 tablespoons chopped fresh thyme
1 tablespoon chopped fresh sage
½ teaspoon sugar

Toss rabbit in flour, shake away excess flour. Heat oil in pan, add rabbit, brown all over, transfer to ovenproof dish (12 cup capacity). Add onion and garlic to same pan, cook, stirring, until onion is soft. Add wine, simmer, uncovered, until almost all liquid has evaporated. Add stock, undrained crushed tomatoes, paste, herbs and sugar, simmer until slightly thickened, pour over rabbit. Bake, covered, in moderate oven about 1½ hours or until rabbit is tender. Serve with bacon lentils and red and green salad.

- ■ Recipe can be made a day ahead.
- ■ Storage: Covered, in refrigerator.
- ■ Freeze: Suitable.
- ■ Microwave: Not suitable.

BACON LENTILS

2 cups (400g) brown lentils
1 tablespoon oil
1 medium (about 150g) onion,
**   chopped**
3 bacon rashers, chopped
2 cloves garlic, crushed
⅔ cup chicken stock
1 tablespoon chopped fresh thyme
2 tablespoons chopped fresh parsley

Place lentils in bowl, cover well with water, stand 1 hour.

Drain lentils, cover with water in pan, simmer about 20 minutes or until just tender; drain. Heat oil in pan, add onion, bacon and garlic, cook, stirring, until onion is lightly browned. Add lentils, stock and thyme, cook, stirring, until liquid is evaporated. Stir in parsley.

- ■ Recipe can be made a day ahead.
- ■ Storage: Covered, in refrigerator.
- ■ Freeze: Suitable.
- ■ Microwave: Suitable.

LEFT: Tangy Tomato Cocktails.
ABOVE LEFT: Vegetable Tempura with Spicy Avocado Sauce.
RIGHT: Herbed Rabbit Casserole with Bacon Lentils.

RED AND GREEN SALAD

1 small red oak leaf lettuce
1 small green oak leaf lettuce
½ small radicchio lettuce
45g snow pea sprouts

DRESSING
½ teaspoon Dijon mustard
1½ tablespoons red wine vinegar
2 tablespoons olive oil
2 tablespoons oil

Tear lettuce into pieces. Combine in bowl with sprouts, toss in dressing.
Dressing: Combine all ingredients in jar; shake well.

■ Salad best made just before serving. Dressing can be made a day ahead.
■ Storage: Covered, in refrigerator.
■ Freeze: Not suitable.

PANETTONE CUSTARD WITH MACERATED FRUIT

½ x 500g panettone
90g soft butter
3 cups milk
300ml carton thickened cream
½ cup castor sugar
1 teaspoon grated orange rind
4cm piece vanilla bean
4 eggs
2 egg yolks
1 tablespoon apricot jam
1 tablespoon Grand Marnier

MACERATED FRUIT
200g raspberries
250g strawberries, halved
200g blueberries
1 medium mango (about 430g), chopped
2 tablespoons castor sugar
¼ cup Kirsch

SOURED CREAM
½ cup thickened cream
⅓ cup sour cream
1 tablespoon icing sugar

Cut panettone into 1cm slices. Toast panettone, spread with butter while hot, cut into fingers. Place fingers of toast in criss-cross pattern into shallow ovenproof dish (6 cup capacity).

Combine milk, cream, sugar, rind and split vanilla bean in pan, stir over heat, without boiling, until sugar is dissolved. Bring to boil, remove from heat, cover, stand 10 minutes; strain.

Beat eggs and egg yolks in bowl, gradually beat in milk mixture. Pour custard over toast. Place dish in baking dish, add enough boiling water to come halfway up sides of ovenproof dish. Bake, uncovered, in moderately slow oven about 1 hour or until lightly browned and firm. Remove from baking dish, brush with combined jam and liqueur. Serve custard warm or cold with macerated fruit and soured cream.

Macerated Fruit: Combine all ingredients in bowl; cover, refrigerate overnight.

Soured Cream: Beat thickened cream in small bowl until soft peaks form, add sour cream and sifted icing sugar, beat until soft peaks form.

■ Macerated fruit best made a day ahead. Panettone custard and soured cream can be made a day ahead.
■ Storage: Covered, in refrigerator.
■ Freeze: Not suitable.
■ Microwave: Not suitable.

ABOVE LEFT: Red and Green Salad.
LEFT AND ABOVE: Panettone Custard with Macerated Fruit.

China from Portmeirion; glassware, tray, serviettes and bread basket from Home & Garden; table and copper pot from Country Furniture Antiques.

Cool Summery Mood

Serves 6

Smoked Chicken Salad with Ginger Crisps

dry to medium-dry rosé

❦

Cold Fish Cutlets with Eggplant Puree

chardonnay or riesling

❦

Tuille Baskets with Berry Sorbet

sparkling rosé

❦

Chocolate Rum Clusters

cognac

❦

Refreshing, cool food with minimum work results in a fuss-free,
do-ahead dinner. The chocolates can be made a week ahead, and
everything else assembled just before serving. We used cold,
smoked chicken for the salad, and added an intriguing touch with
fresh ginger crisps. For the cold fish course, use any firm white fish
that holds its shape and texture in cooking. And for dessert, the
biscuit baskets for the beautifully flavoured sorbet are quite easy to
shape if you handle them quickly.

ABOVE: Smoked Chicken Salad with Ginger Crisps.
RIGHT: Cold Fish Cutlets with Eggplant Puree.

SMOKED CHICKEN SALAD WITH GINGER CRISPS

12 fresh asparagus spears, halved
1 radicchio lettuce
1 green oak leaf lettuce
3 single smoked chicken breast
    fillets, thinly sliced

RASPBERRY DRESSING
½ cup olive oil
⅓ cup raspberry vinegar
1 clove garlic, crushed
¼ teaspoon sugar
2 teaspoons chopped fresh parsley
1 egg yolk
¼ cup grated parmesan cheese

GINGER CRISPS
1 medium (about 150g) piece fresh
    ginger root
icing sugar
oil for deep-frying

CROUTONS
4 slices white bread
40g butter, melted

Boil, steam or microwave asparagus until just tender, drain; rinse under cold water, drain. Tear lettuce into pieces, combine with asparagus, chicken, raspberry dressing and croutons in bowl; toss well. Sprinkle salad with ginger crisps just before serving.
Raspberry Dressing: Combine all ingredients in jar; shake well.
Ginger Crisps: Peel ginger, peel thin strips from ginger using vegetable peeler. Toss ginger in icing sugar. Deep-fry ginger in hot oil until lightly browned; drain on absorbent paper.
Croutons: Remove crusts from bread. Brush both sides of bread with butter. Cut bread into quarters, cut each quarter diagonally into 2 triangles. Place on oven tray in single layer. Toast in moderate oven for 10 minutes; cool.

- Dressing and croutons can be made 2 days ahead. Ginger crisps can be made an hour ahead. Assemble salad just before serving.
- Storage: Dressing, croutons and ginger crisps separately, in airtight containers.
- Freeze: Croutons suitable.
- Microwave: Asparagus suitable.

COLD FISH CUTLETS WITH EGGPLANT PUREE

6 x 250g jewfish cutlets
2 tablespoons olive oil
⅓ cup dry white wine
2 tablespoons lemon juice

EGGPLANT PUREE
2 large (about 940g) eggplants
2 tablespoons olive oil
2 cloves garlic, crushed
2 teaspoons chopped fresh thyme
1 tablespoon lemon juice
¼ cup mayonnaise
¼ teaspoon sugar

TOMATO DRESSING
3 medium (about 390g) tomatoes,
    peeled, seeded
6 small (about 390g) zucchini, finely
    chopped
¼ cup chopped fresh basil
2 tablespoons lemon juice
½ cup olive oil
¼ cup virgin olive oil

Place fish on oven tray, brush with oil, pour over wine and juice, cover, bake in moderate oven about 20 minutes or until fish is just tender. Transfer fish and liquid to glass dish, cover, cool, refrigerate.

Just before serving, drain fish, serve on eggplant puree with tomato dressing.
Eggplant Puree: Halve eggplants lengthways, make diagonal cuts 2cm apart across the cut sides. Place eggplant halves on oven tray, brush with oil, cover, bake in moderate oven about 1¼ hours or until eggplants are very soft. Scoop out pulp, discard skins. Process eggplant pulp, garlic, thyme, juice, mayonnaise and sugar until smooth.
Tomato Dressing: Combine finely chopped tomatoes with remaining ingredients in bowl.

- Recipe can be prepared a day ahead.
- Storage: Separately, covered, in refrigerator.
- Freeze: Not suitable.
- Microwave: Fish suitable.

TUILLE BASKETS WITH BERRY SORBET

200g blueberries
125g strawberries, halved
125g raspberries

TUILLE BASKETS
2 egg whites
½ cup castor sugar
⅓ cup plain flour
60g butter, melted
2 teaspoons vanilla essence
½ cup flaked almonds, approximately

BERRY SORBET
1½ cups castor sugar
3 cups water
300g raspberries
250g strawberries
3 egg whites

BERRY SAUCE
125g strawberries
125g raspberries
½ cup orange juice
1 tablespoon icing sugar

Mix berries with ¼ cup berry sauce; divide berry mixture between tuille baskets. Top baskets with scoops of sorbet.
Tuille Baskets: Lightly grease 2 oven trays. Beat egg whites in small bowl with electric mixer until soft peaks form, gradually beat in sugar, beat until dis-solved. Fold in sifted flour, butter and essence. Spread 2½ tablespoons of mixture onto prepared trays, spread to 17cm rounds. Sprinkle with about 3 teaspoons of nuts. Bake 1 tuille at a time in moderate oven about 7 minutes or until lightly browned. Remove carefully from tray with spatula while still warm. Shape quickly around inverted tall glass; leave to set. You will need 6 tuille baskets.
Berry Sorbet: Combine sugar and water in pan, stir over heat, without boiling, until sugar is dissolved; simmer, uncovered, without stirring, 10 minutes; cool. Blend or process sugar syrup and berries until smooth; strain. Place berry mixture in shallow pan, cover, freeze until just firm. Chop berry mixture; process with egg whites until smooth. Return to pan, cover; freeze until firm.
Berry Sauce: Blend or process all ingredients until smooth; strain.

- ■ Berry sorbet can be made a week ahead. Tuille baskets and berry sauce can be made a day ahead.
- ■ Storage: Berry sorbet, covered, in freezer. Tuille baskets, in airtight container. Berry sauce, covered, in refrigerator.
- ■ Freeze: Berry sorbet essential. Berry sauce suitable.
- ■ Microwave: Not suitable.

CHOCOLATE RUM CLUSTERS

2 tablespoons sultanas
2 teaspoons dark rum
60g dark chocolate, chopped
2 tablespoons cream
2 tablespoons chopped macadamias

Combine sultanas and rum in bowl, cover, stand several hours or overnight.

Combine chocolate and cream in bowl, stir over low heat until melted. Stir in undrained sultanas and nuts. Divide mixture between 12 small foil cases, refrigerate until set.

Makes 12.

- ■ Chocolate rum clusters can be made a week ahead.
- ■ Storage: Covered, in refrigerator.
- ■ Freeze: Suitable.
- ■ Microwave: Suitable.

LEFT: Tuillle Baskets with Berry Sorbet.
BELOW: Chocolate Rum Clusters.

China and glassware from Villeroy & Boch; cutlery from Gero; silver tray and cane tray from Corso de Fiori; chairs from Country Furniture Antiques.

Spring Elegance

Serves 6

Dill Blinis with Smoked Seafood Pate
dry white burgundy or chablis
❦

Lamb Fillets with Creamy Pesto
Mustardy Baked Potatoes with Olives
Shredded Green Vegetables
pinot noir, beaujolais or chianti
❦

Lime Bavarois with Passionfruit Jelly
sweet sparkling wine or late-picked riesling
❦

Light, fresh and elegant, this is a lovely dinner for spring when lamb is at its best. Hot blinis, or yeasty pancakes, are a tempting entree with smoked salmon, do-ahead seafood pate and creme fraiche. The lamb is simplicity itself; you remove the centres from cutlet racks, cook as desired and serve with an easy sauce, mixed green vegetables and baked potatoes with mustard and olives. A light bavarois follows; it's best made a day ahead.

DILL BLINIS WITH SMOKED SEAFOOD PATE

12 slices smoked salmon
6 sprigs fresh dill

SMOKED SEAFOOD PATE
250g smoked trout
200g smoked eel
10g butter
1 small onion, chopped
1½ teaspoons Dijon mustard
3 teaspoons horseradish cream
80g soft butter, extra

DILL BLINIS
2 teaspoons (7g) dried yeast
½ teaspoon sugar
⅔ cup warm milk
1 egg, separated
1 egg yolk
½ cup sour cream
1 cup plain flour
½ teaspoon salt
2 tablespoons chopped fresh dill
½ small green pepper, finely chopped

CREME FRAICHE
⅔ cup sour cream
⅔ cup thickened cream

Place 2 slices of salmon on each plate, serve with sliced smoked seafood pate, dill blinis, creme fraiche and dill sprigs.

Smoked Seafood Pate: Oil 2 mini loaf pans (¾ cup capacity), line bases and sides with greaseproof paper, oil paper. Remove skin from trout and eel, remove flesh from bones; cut flesh into pieces.

Heat butter in pan, add onion, cook, stirring, until onion is soft. Process trout, eel and onion mixture until combined. Add remaining ingredients, process until smooth. Spoon mixture into prepared pans, cover, refrigerate until set. Turn pate out of pans, cut into 12 slices.

Dill Blinis: Combine yeast, sugar and half the milk in small bowl, cover, stand in warm place about 10 minutes or until mixture is frothy. Stir in combined egg yolks, sour cream and remaining milk.

Sift flour and salt into large bowl. Gradually stir sour cream mixture into flour mixture, stir until mixture is smooth; cover, stand in warm place about 1 hour or until batter rises and is slightly bubbly.

Beat egg white in small bowl until firm peaks form. Fold egg white, dill and pepper into batter, cover, stand in warm place

about 2 hours or until mixture is bubbly. Spoon 1½ tablespoons of batter into heated greased heavy-based pan; cook until lightly browned underneath. Turn blinis, brown other side. Repeat with remaining batter. You will need 12 blinis for this recipe.

Creme Fraiche: Combine both creams in bowl, cover, stand at room temperature until mixture has thickened. This can take 1 to 2 days, depending on the room temperature. Cover creme fraiche, refrigerate before serving.

- ■ Smoked seafood pate and creme fraiche can be made 2 days ahead. Blinis best made just before serving.
- ■ Storage: Covered, in refrigerator.
- ■ Freeze: Not suitable.
- ■ Microwave: Not suitable.

LAMB FILLETS WITH CREAMY PESTO

4 racks of lamb (6 cutlets each)
2 teaspoons oil
15g butter

CREAMY PESTO
1 cup firmly packed fresh basil leaves
1 clove garlic, crushed
⅓ cup pine nuts, toasted
1 teaspoon olive oil
¼ cup grated parmesan cheese
1 cup thickened cream

Carefully remove the long piece of meat in each rack without cutting through bones; discard bones. Heat oil and butter in baking dish, add lamb, cook over high heat until lamb is browned all over. Bake, uncovered, in moderate oven for about 10 minutes or until lamb is cooked as desired; cover, stand 5 minutes before slicing. Serve lamb fillets with creamy pesto, shredded green vegetables and mustardy baked potatoes with olives.
Creamy Pesto: Blend or process basil, garlic, pine nuts, oil and cheese until well combined. Combine basil mixture and cream in pan, simmer, uncovered, for about 5 minutes or until slightly thickened.

■ Recipe best made just before serving.
■ Freeze: Not suitable.
■ Microwave: Not suitable.

MUSTARDY BAKED POTATOES WITH OLIVES

6 large (about 1.5kg) potatoes
⅓ cup olive oil
1 medium (about 150g) onion, finely chopped
2 cloves garlic, crushed
2 teaspoons black mustard seeds
2 teaspoons dry mustard
1 tablespoon dried Italian herbs
½ cup sliced black olives

Cut potatoes into 2cm pieces. Heat oil in large baking dish, add potatoes, onion, garlic, mustard seeds, dry mustard and herbs; stir over heat until combined. Bake, uncovered, in moderately hot oven 30 minutes, stir in olives, bake further 30 minutes, uncovered, or until potatoes are browned and crisp.

■ Recipe best made close to serving.
■ Freeze: Not suitable.
■ Microwave: Not suitable.

SHREDDED GREEN VEGETABLES

1 large (about 150g) zucchini
125g snow peas, sliced
3 fresh asparagus spears, sliced
200g broccoli, chopped

Cut zucchini into long thin strips. Boil, steam or microwave green vegetables until just tender.

■ Recipe best made close to serving.
■ Freeze: Not suitable.
■ Microwave: Suitable.

LEFT: Dill Blinis with Smoked Seafood Pate.
ABOVE: Lamb Fillets with Creamy Pesto, Shredded Green Vegetables and Mustardy Baked Potatoes with Olives.

ABOVE: Lime Bavarois with Passionfruit Jelly.

China and glassware from Waterford Wedgwood; cutlery from Georg Jensen; tablecloth and serviettes from The Bay Tree.

LIME BAVAROIS WITH PASSIONFRUIT JELLY

1 egg, separated
2 teaspoons castor sugar
½ teaspoon vanilla essence
3 teaspoons castor sugar, extra
1 tablespoon self-raising flour

LIME BAVAROIS
3 egg yolks
½ cup castor sugar
1 cup milk
1 teaspoon grated lime rind
½ cup lime juice
2½ teaspoons gelatine
300ml carton thickened cream

PASSIONFRUIT JELLY
12 passionfruit
¼ cup water
1 tablespoon icing sugar
2 teaspoons gelatine

For sponge layer, grease and flour oven tray, mark 21cm circle on tray. Beat egg yolk and sugar in small bowl with electric mixer until thick, add essence. Beat egg white in small bowl until soft peaks form, beat in extra sugar, beat until dissolved. Fold sifted flour into egg yolk mixture, gently fold in egg white mixture.

Spread mixture onto prepared tray, using circle as guide. Bake in moderate oven about 10 minutes or until sponge is cooked through. Turn sponge layer onto wire rack to cool.

Trim sponge layer to fit into 20cm springform tin.

Pour lime bavarois over sponge layer in tin, cover, refrigerate about 2 hours or until firm. Pour passionfruit jelly over lime bavarois, cover, refrigerate several hours or overnight.

Lime Bavarois: Beat egg yolks and sugar in small bowl with electric mixer until thick and creamy. Heat milk in pan, bring to boil. Gradually beat hot milk into egg yolk mixture while motor is operating. Pour mixture into pan, stir over low heat, without boiling, until custard mixture is slightly thickened. Stir in rind and ⅓ cup of the lime juice.

Sprinkle gelatine over remaining juice in cup, stand in pan of simmering water, stir until dissolved; pour into lime mixture; cover, cool, refrigerate 1 hour or until mixture is almost set. Beat cream in small bowl until soft peaks form, gently fold into lime mixture.

Passionfruit Jelly: Remove pulp from passionfruit. Strain pulp, reserve juice and seeds; you will need ½ cup juice and 1 tablespoon seeds. Combine reserved juice and seeds in pan, add water and icing sugar. Bring to boil, remove from heat, add gelatine, stir until dissolved. Cool to room temperature.

■ Recipe best made a day ahead.
■ Storage: Covered, in refrigerator.
■ Freeze: Not suitable.
■ Microwave: Gelatine mixtures suitable.

A Winter's Table

Serves 6

Creamy Leek, Fennel and Potato Soup
Corn Bread Rolls

chilled dry sherry

**Lamb Shanks with Beans
and Tomatoes**

Buttery Braised Cabbage

cabernet sauvignon or cabernet merlot

**Warm Date Pudding with
Butterscotch Sauce**

auslese riesling

On a cold winter's night, this hearty, generous feast is a welcome sight. The creamy soup,

thick with fennel, leeks and potato, can be made ahead, as can the corn bread rolls.

Then comes the surprise: inexpensive lamb shanks simmered to terrific flavour

and tenderness in rich-tasting wine sauce. They're best cooked ahead, but the

buttery cabbage is cooked just before serving. Topping it all off is a date pudding

lavished with butterscotch sauce; both can be made ahead, too.

CREAMY LEEK, FENNEL AND POTATO SOUP

Fresh dill may be used if tops of fennel are not attached to bulbs.

1 medium (about 450g) fennel bulb
30g butter
3 small (about 600g) leeks, sliced
1 clove garlic, crushed
1 large (about 250g) potato, chopped

1.5 litres (6 cups) water
2 teaspoons chicken stock powder
1 bay leaf
¼ cup chopped fresh chives
¼ cup cream

Slice fennel bulb, reserve 1 tablespoon of chopped fennel tops. Heat butter in pan, add fennel bulb, leeks and garlic, cook, stirring, until fennel is soft. Add potato, cook, stirring, further 5 minutes. Stir in water, stock powder and bay leaf, simmer, covered, 30 minutes. Discard bay leaf, blend or process soup in batches until smooth. Return soup to pan, stir in chives, reserved chopped fennel tops and cream, stir over heat until hot.

■ Soup can be made a day ahead.
■ Storage: Covered, in refrigerator.
■ Freeze: Suitable.
■ Microwave: Suitable.

CORN BREAD ROLLS

2 teaspoons (7g) dried yeast
½ cup warm water
2 teaspoons brown sugar
2 cups white plain flour
¼ cup wholemeal plain flour
½ cup cornmeal
½ teaspoon salt
⅔ cup warm milk
2 teaspoons cornmeal, extra

Combine yeast, water and sugar in bowl, stand in warm place about 10 minutes or until frothy. Sift flours into bowl. Stir cornmeal, salt, milk and yeast mixture into flour; mix to a soft dough. Knead dough on floured surface about 5 minutes or until smooth and elastic. Place dough in oiled bowl, cover, stand in warm place about 45 minutes or until doubled in size.

Divide dough into 6 portions. Knead each portion for 2 minutes, shape portions into rolls. Place rolls on greased oven trays. Flatten rolls slightly, cut a shallow cross in top of each roll, sprinkle with extra cornmeal. Stand in warm place about 30 minutes or until almost doubled in size. Bake in moderately hot oven about 20 minutes or until rolls are browned and sound hollow when tapped.

Makes 6.

■ Recipe can be made several hours ahead.
■ Storage: Covered, at room temperature
■ Freeze: Suitable.
■ Microwave: Not suitable.

LAMB SHANKS WITH BEANS AND TOMATOES

¾ cup dried haricot beans
6 medium lamb shanks
plain flour
¼ cup oil
2 medium (about 340g) red Spanish onions, sliced
2 teaspoons cumin seeds
4 cloves garlic, sliced
2 cups chicken stock
1 cup dry red wine
6 large (about 1.5kg) tomatoes, peeled, seeded
425g can tomato puree
2 teaspoons sugar
6 large sprigs fresh rosemary
3 bay leaves

Place beans in bowl, cover with water, cover, stand overnight. Drain beans, discard water. Place beans in pan, cover with fresh water, simmer, partly covered, 30 minutes; drain.

Toss lamb in flour, shake away excess flour. Heat half the oil in large pan, add lamb in 2 batches, cook until browned all over; remove from pan. Heat remaining oil in same pan, add onions, seeds and garlic, cook, stirring, until onions are soft. Add lamb, stock, wine, chopped tomatoes, puree, sugar, rosemary, bay leaves and beans. Simmer, partly covered, about 1¼ hours or until beans and lamb are tender. Discard bay leaves. Serve lamb with buttery braised cabbage.

■ Recipe can be made 3 days ahead.
■ Storage: Covered, in refrigerator.
■ Freeze: Suitable.
■ Microwave: Suitable.

BUTTERY BRAISED CABBAGE

90g butter
½ medium (about 750g) cabbage, shredded
⅓ cup dry white wine
½ cup chicken stock
1 teaspoon seasoned pepper

Heat butter in large pan, add cabbage, cook, stirring, until cabbage is softened. Add wine, stock and pepper, cover, cook over low heat about 5 minutes or until cabbage is just tender.

■ Cabbage best cooked close to serving.
■ Freeze: Not suitable.
■ Microwave: Suitable.

LEFT: Creamy Leek, Fennel and Potato Soup with Corn Bread Rolls.
BELOW: Lamb Shanks with Beans and Tomatoes and Buttery Braised Cabbage.

WARM DATE PUDDING WITH BUTTERSCOTCH SAUCE

1¼ cups (200g) chopped dates
1¼ cups water
1 teaspoon bicarbonate of soda
60g butter
¾ cup castor sugar
2 eggs
1 cup self-raising flour

BUTTERSCOTCH SAUCE
1 cup (200g) brown sugar,
**   firmly packed**
1 cup cream
200g butter

Grease deep 20cm round cake pan. Line base with paper, grease paper. Combine dates and water in pan, bring to boil, remove from heat, add soda, stand 5 minutes. Blend or process until smooth.

Cream butter and sugar in small bowl with electric mixer until well combined. Beat in eggs 1 at a time. Gently fold in sifted flour, then date mixture. Pour mixture into prepared pan, bake in moderate oven about 55 minutes or until cooked through. Cover pudding with foil if it becomes too dark during cooking. Stand pudding 10 minutes before turning onto wire rack over oven tray. Pour ¼ cup sauce over pudding, return to moderate oven, bake, uncovered, further 5 minutes. Serve pudding with remaining sauce.

Butterscotch Sauce: Combine all ingredients in pan, stir over heat, without boiling, until sugar is dissolved, then simmer, stirring, 3 minutes.

■ Recipe can be made a day ahead.
■ Storage: Pudding, in airtight container. Sauce, covered, in refrigerator.
■ Freeze: Pudding suitable.
■ Microwave: Dates and sauce suitable.

ABOVE: Warm Date Pudding with Butterscotch Sauce.

China from Villeroy & Boch; cutlery from The Bay Tree; glasses and salt cellar from Accoutrement; tablecloth from Aginian's.

Mediterranean Flavours

Serves 8

Kumara Crisps
dry sparkling wine

❧

Warm Squid Salad with Sweet Onions
gewurztraminer or young riesling

❧

**Racks of Lamb with Hummus
and Couscous**
cabernet sauvignon merlot blend

❧

**Apricot Brioche with
Glazed Fresh Apricots**
sweet white botrytis wine

❧

Start the party with our golden kumara crisps; they're extra yummy, lightly salted and irresistible for nibbling! Then move on to the delicate Mediterranean flavours of squid salad, rosemary lamb racks, hummus and couscous. The crisps can be made 2 days ahead, but the squid, lamb, zucchini and couscous are best cooked just before serving. Hummus needs no cooking, and can be made 3 days ahead. For dessert, the apricot brioche and luscious, syrupy apricots are easy to assemble just before serving.

WARM SQUID SALAD WITH SWEET ONIONS

1 medium (about 200g) red pepper
1 butter lettuce
1 coral lettuce
6 large (about 800g) squid hoods
½ cup dry white wine
2 cloves garlic, crushed
1 tablespoon brown sugar
2 tablespoons olive oil

DRESSING
½ cup olive oil
⅓ cup lemon juice
1 tablespoon red wine vinegar
2 teaspoons honey

SWEET ONIONS
⅓ cup olive oil
5 large (about 1kg) red Spanish onions, sliced
⅓ cup brown sugar

KUMARA CRISPS

2 large (about 1.1kg) kumara
oil for deep-frying

SEASONED SALT
½ teaspoon onion salt
½ teaspoon celery salt
½ teaspoon paprika
½ teaspoon ground cumin

Using vegetable peeler, peel strips lengthways from kumara. Deep-fry quarter of the strips in hot oil about 7 minutes or until strips are lightly browned; drain on absorbent paper. Repeat with remaining strips. Kumara strips become crisp on cooling.

Just before serving, sprinkle with seasoned salt.
Seasoned Salt: Combine all ingredients in bowl; mix well.

■ Recipe can be made 2 days ahead.
■ Storage: In airtight container.
■ Freeze: Not suitable.
■ Microwave: Not suitable.

Cut pepper into fine strips. Tear lettuce leaves into large pieces. Cut a criss-cross pattern on inner side of squid hoods; do not cut all the way through. Cut squid into 2cm x 5cm strips. Combine squid, wine, garlic and sugar in bowl, cover, refrigerate for 1 hour.

Just before serving, drain squid, discard marinade. Heat oil in pan, add squid, cook about 2 minutes or until curled and tender; stir in pepper, cook further 30 seconds. Toss half the dressing through

lettuce leaves, place on serving plates, top with sweet onions, then warm squid; drizzle with remaining dressing.

Dressing: Combine all ingredients in jar; shake well.

Sweet Onions: Heat oil in pan, add onions, cook, covered, over low heat 30 minutes, stirring occasionally. Stir in sugar, stir over heat until sugar is dissolved and onions are golden; cool.

- Recipe best made just before serving.
- Freeze: Not suitable.
- Microwave: Not suitable.

RACKS OF LAMB WITH HUMMUS AND COUSCOUS

8 racks of lamb cutlets (3 cutlets each)
1 tablespoon olive oil
1 tablespoon chopped fresh rosemary
1½ tablespoons plain flour
¼ cup dry red wine
1¼ cups beef stock
6 small (about 390g) zucchini
1 tablespoon olive oil, extra
2 tablespoons chopped fresh chives

HUMMUS
425g can chick peas, rinsed, drained
¼ cup tahini
⅓ cup lemon juice
3 cloves garlic, crushed
⅔ cup water

COUSCOUS
1½ cups (270g) couscous
1¼ cups boiling water
80g butter
1 small (about 150g) red pepper, finely chopped
2 tablespoons chopped fresh parsley

Trim excess fat from lamb, place lamb on wire rack in baking dish, brush with oil, sprinkle with rosemary. Bake, uncovered, in moderate oven about 30 minutes or until tender. Remove lamb from dish; keep warm. Add flour to same dish, cook, stirring, until flour is browned. Remove from heat, gradually stir in wine and stock. Stir over heat until sauce boils and thickens; strain. Cut zucchini lengthways into thin slices, brush with extra oil.

Just before serving, cook zucchini on griddle pan or grill until just tender, sprinkle with chives. Cut lamb racks into cutlets, serve with zucchini, hummus, couscous, and sauce.

Hummus: Blend or process all ingredients until smooth.

Couscous: Place couscous in bowl, add boiling water, stand about 2 minutes or until all water is absorbed.

Just before serving, heat butter in pan, add couscous, cook, stirring, until grains are tender; stir in pepper and parsley.

- Lamb, zucchini and couscous must be cooked just before serving. Hummus can be made 3 days ahead.
- Storage: Covered, in refrigerator.
- Freeze: Not suitable.
- Microwave: Couscous suitable.

ABOVE LEFT: Kumara Crisps.
LEFT: Warm Squid Salad with Sweet Onions.
ABOVE: Racks of Lamb with Hummus and Couscous.

apricots. Stir in yeast mixture, mix to a firm dough. Turn dough onto floured surface, knead about 5 minutes or until dough is smooth. Gradually knead in small pieces of soft butter, knead until smooth (this will take about 10 minutes). Place dough into large greased bowl, cover, stand in warm place about 1 hour or until dough is doubled in size.

Turn dough onto floured surface, knead for 1 minute. Divide dough into 8 portions, cut one-third of dough off each portion. Roll large portions into balls and place into prepared tins. Roll small portions into balls, place 1 on top of each large ball. Push a skewer through both balls through to bases of tins to secure balls together; remove skewer.

Cover brioche, stand in warm place for about 30 minutes or until doubled in size. Brush brioche lightly with combined extra yolks and extra milk. Bake in moderately hot oven 10 minutes, reduce heat to moderate, bake about further 10 minutes or until brioche are golden brown (cover tops with foil if becoming too dark).

Remove brioche from oven, stand 5 minutes, remove from tins. Serve brioche with glazed fresh apricots, cardamom syrup and spiced mascarpone.

Glazed Fresh Apricots: Combine sugar and water in pan, stir over heat, without boiling, until sugar is dissolved. Add apricots, simmer, uncovered, without stirring, 2 minutes, remove from heat; cool. Refrigerate apricots in sugar syrup.

Just before serving, drain apricots, discard sugar syrup.

Cardamom Syrup: Combine sugar, water, cinnamon and cardamom in pan, stir over heat, without boiling, until sugar is dissolved. Simmer, uncovered, about 10 minutes, without stirring, or until syrup is thick. Stir in brandy; strain, cool to cold.

Spiced Mascarpone: Combine all ingredients in bowl, beat until smooth.

- Brioche can be made several hours ahead. Apricots; cardamom syrup and spiced mascarpone can be prepared a day ahead.
- Storage: Covered, in refrigerator.
- Freeze: Brioche suitable.
- Microwave: Not suitable.

APRICOT BRIOCHE WITH GLAZED FRESH APRICOTS

15g compressed yeast
2 tablespoons castor sugar
⅔ cup warm milk
3 egg yolks
2 cups plain flour
⅔ cup chopped dried apricots
100g unsalted butter
2 egg yolks, extra
1 tablespoon milk, extra

GLAZED FRESH APRICOTS
1½ cups castor sugar
3 cups water
16 medium (about 800g) fresh apricots

CARDAMOM SYRUP
2 cups castor sugar
1 cup water
1 cinnamon stick
2 cardamom pods, crushed
1 tablespoon brandy

SPICED MASCARPONE
500g mascarpone cheese
½ teaspoon ground cardamom
2 tablespoons icing sugar

Grease 8 x 7cm fluted flan tins. Cream yeast and 1 teaspoon of the sugar in bowl; stir in milk, cover, stand in warm place about 15 minutes or until mixture is frothy.

Stir yolks into yeast mixture. Sift flour into large bowl, stir in remaining sugar and

ABOVE LEFT: Apricot Brioche with Glazed Fresh Apricots.

China from Royal Doulton.

A Touch of Class

Serves 6

**Pumpkin Ravioli with Creamy
Herb Sauce**

chardonnay

**Salmon Fillets with Sweet and
Sour Onions**

Potato Sails

Saute Spinach

full-flavoured chardonnay

**Shortbread with Lemon Curd
and Candied Rind**

orange muscat or late-picked
spatlese riesling

Light in taste and texture, and using first-rate fresh ingredients, this special-occasion dinner
needs extra time just before serving, as almost everything is made then. The ravioli are
rolled, filled, cooked and sauced. Then it's on to salmon fillets, easy in the griddle pan, and
served with made-ahead onion relish, saute spinach and deep-fried potatoes (the sails are
simply slices shaped with toothpicks). For dessert, shortbread melts deliciously against
lemon curd and candied rind, all ready to assemble.

PUMPKIN RAVIOLI WITH CREAMY HERB SAUCE

It is important to use 60g eggs for this pasta. You will need about 400g pumpkin.

¼ cup pepitas (pumpkin seed kernels)

PASTA
2 cups plain flour
3 eggs, lightly beaten

FILLING
¾ cup cooked mashed pumpkin
⅔ cup ricotta cheese
⅓ cup grated parmesan cheese
½ teaspoon seasoned pepper
pinch ground nutmeg

CREAMY HERB SAUCE
1 cup dry white wine
4 black peppercorns
1 clove garlic, sliced
4 green shallots, chopped
1 bay leaf
300ml carton cream
2 teaspoons seeded mustard
1 tablespoon chopped fresh tarragon
1 tablespoon chopped fresh basil
1 tablespoon chopped fresh chives

Add ravioli to large pan of boiling water, simmer, uncovered, about 5 minutes or until just tender; drain. Serve ravioli with creamy herb sauce and pepitas.

Pasta: Process flour and eggs until mixture forms a ball. Knead dough on lightly floured surface until smooth. Cut dough in half, roll each half through pasta machine set on thickest setting.

Fold dough in half, roll through machine. Repeat rolling and folding several times or until dough is smooth and elastic; dust dough with a little extra flour when necessary. Continue rolling dough through machine, adjusting setting to become less thick with each roll; dust dough with a little extra flour when necessary. Roll to 1mm thickness.

Cut dough into 10cm strips. Place 2 level teaspoons of filling 6cm apart over 1 strip of pasta. Brush in between filling with water; top with another strip of pasta. Press firmly between filling and along edges of pasta. Cut into square ravioli shapes. Repeat with remaining pasta and filling. Lightly sprinkle ravioli with flour.

Filling: Combine all ingredients in bowl; mix well.

Creamy Herb Sauce: Combine wine, peppercorns, garlic, shallots and bay leaf in pan, simmer, uncovered, until reduced to ½ cup; strain. Combine reduced wine liquid, cream and mustard in pan, simmer, uncovered, until slightly thickened; stir in fresh herbs.

- Recipe best made close to serving.
- Freeze: Uncooked ravioli suitable.
- Microwave: Suitable.

SALMON FILLETS WITH SWEET AND SOUR ONIONS

6 (about 1.2kg) salmon fillets

SWEET AND SOUR ONIONS
40g butter
2 medium (about 300g) onions, sliced
2 tablespoons water
⅓ cup brown sugar
½ cup brown vinegar
2 tablespoons raisins
½ teaspoon grated orange rind

Cook salmon on both sides on lightly oiled griddle pan or grill until tender. Serve with sweet and sour onions, potato sails and saute spinach.

Sweet and Sour Onions: Heat butter in pan, add onions; stir until onions are coated in butter. Add water, cover, cook over low heat about 15 minutes, stirring occasionally, or until onions are soft. Add sugar, vinegar and raisins, simmer about further 15 minutes or until liquid has thickened; stir in rind. Serve warm.

- Sweet and sour onions can be made 4 days ahead.
- Storage: Covered, in refrigerator.
- Freeze: Not suitable.
- Microwave: Suitable.

POTATO SAILS

3 large (about 600g) old potatoes
oil for deep-frying
1 teaspoon salt
pinch paprika

Wash potatoes, cut into very thin slices across width; slice only 1 potato at a time to prevent discolouring. Layer 3 slices of potato together, push toothpicks through outside edges to form a "U" shape. Deep-fry potatoes in hot oil until lightly browned; drain on absorbent paper. Re-fry potatoes in reheated oil until golden brown; drain on absorbent paper, sprinkle with combined salt and paprika; remove toothpicks.

- Recipe must be made just before serving.
- Freeze: Not suitable.
- Microwave: Not suitable.

SAUTE SPINACH

60g butter
2 bunches (about 1.3kg) English
   spinach
¼ teaspoon ground nutmeg

Heat butter in pan, add spinach and nutmeg, toss over high heat until wilted.

- Spinach best cooked just before serving.
- Freeze: Suitable.
- Microwave: Suitable.

LEFT: Pumpkin Ravioli with Creamy Herb Sauce.
ABOVE: Salmon Fillets with Sweet and Sour Onions, Potato Sails and Saute Spinach.

SHORTBREAD WITH LEMON CURD AND CANDIED RIND

1⅓ cups plain flour
½ cup icing sugar
200g butter
2 egg yolks
¼ teaspoon vanilla essence
icing sugar, extra

LEMON CURD
3 eggs
¾ cup castor sugar
3 teaspoons grated lemon rind
⅓ cup lemon juice
125g butter, chopped

CANDIED RIND
4 medium (about 520g) lemons
2 medium (about 600g) grapefruit
1½ cups castor sugar
1½ cups water

Lightly grease 2 large oven trays. Sift flour and sugar into bowl, rub in butter, gently stir in combined egg yolks and essence until just combined. Form mixture into ball, cover, refrigerate 2 hours.

Remove dough from refrigerator, stand 10 minutes. Roll out half the dough between sheets of baking paper until 2mm thick. Place on tray, cover, refrigerate until firm. Repeat with remaining dough.

Cut 9 x 8cm rounds from each piece of dough, place about 5cm apart on prepared trays, bake in slow oven about 30 minutes or until lightly browned. Cool on tray 5 minutes before transferring to rack to cool completely.

Place 1 shortbread on each serving plate, top with a heaped tablespoon of lemon curd and a teaspoon of candied rind. Repeat layering once more, finishing with shortbread. Dust with extra sifted icing sugar. Decorate with more candied rind and a little of the syrup.

Lemon Curd: Combine eggs, sugar, rind and juice in pan, stir over low heat, without boiling, until mixture is thick. Transfer to bowl, whisk in butter a little at a time; cool. Cover bowl, refrigerate.

Candied Rind: Peel rind thinly from lemons and grapefruit with vegetable peeler, cut rind into thin strips. Place rind in pan, cover with water, bring to boil, drain; repeat twice.

Place sugar and water in pan, stir over heat, without boiling, until sugar is dissolved, simmer 1 minute. Add rind, simmer over heat, without stirring, about 10 minutes or until rind is clear; cool.

- Shortbread, lemon curd and candied rind can be made 2 days ahead.
- Storage: Shortbread, in airtight container. Lemon curd and candied rind, covered, in refrigerator.
- Freeze: Shortbread suitable.
- Microwave: Candied rind suitable.

LEFT: Shortbread with Lemon Curd and Candied Rind.

China and glassware from Waterford Wedgwood; fabric from Les Olivades.

Indian Vegetarian Banquet

Serves 10

Spiced Nutty Nibbles

Corn and Pea Samosas

semillon

Vegetables and Cashew Curry

Ricotta Dumplings in Chilli Spinach Sauce

Flat Poppyseed Bread

Aromatic Rice

Chick Pea Salad

Coriander Dhal

Mango Chutney

Cucumber Raita

gewurztraminer or medium-dry moselle-style

Date Syrup Pancakes

chilled tawny port

Whether you're vegetarian or not, you'll enjoy this combination of spicy, enticing tastes put together with an Indian flavour. Don't be deterred by the number of dishes, because most can be done in advance and heated up on the day. The curry actually improves with being made ahead! Soon before serving, you mix the cucumber and yogurt raita, make the flat poppyseed bread (allow proving time for this), and mix and cook the pancakes for the delicious dessert with a difference.

SPICED NUTTY NIBBLES

½ cup raw peanuts
½ cup raw cashews
oil for deep-frying
4 cups (80g) puffed rice
½ cup sultanas
6 large pappadams
2 tablespoons oil, extra
2 teaspoons black mustard seeds
¼ cup sesame seeds
2 small fresh green chillies, sliced
¼ teaspoon turmeric
½ teaspoon garam masala
pinch ground cloves
pinch ground cinnamon
pinch cayenne pepper
2 teaspoons fine sea salt
2 teaspoons castor sugar

Rub brown skins off peanuts. Deep-fry cashews in hot oil until lightly browned, drain on absorbent paper; repeat with peanuts. Deep-fry rice in hot oil in batches until lightly browned, drain on absorbent paper. Deep-fry sultanas and pappadams in hot oil until both are puffed, drain on absorbent paper.

Meanwhile, heat extra oil in pan, add mustard and sesame seeds, chillies and spices, cook, stirring, until seeds are lightly browned and mixture is aromatic. Remove from pan; cool.

Combine cashews and peanuts, rice, sultanas, broken pappadams, sesame seed mixture, salt and sugar in bowl.

- Recipe can be made 2 days ahead.
- Storage: Airtight container.
- Freeze: Not suitable.
- Microwave: Not suitable.

CORN AND PEA SAMOSAS

1½ cups plain flour
30g ghee
1 tablespoon cumin seeds
½ cup warm water, approximately
oil for deep-frying

FILLING
10g ghee
½ small onion, finely chopped
1 clove garlic, crushed
1 teaspoon grated fresh ginger
1 teaspoon cumin seeds
1 teaspoon coriander seeds
2 teaspoons garam masala
¼ teaspoon turmeric
¼ teaspoon chilli powder
⅔ cup drained canned corn kernels
⅔ cup frozen peas, thawed
¼ cup coconut cream

Sift flour into bowl, rub in ghee, add seeds, gradually stir in enough water to mix to a firm dough. Knead on lightly floured surface for about 5 minutes or until smooth. Cover, refrigerate 30 minutes.

Roll pastry on lightly floured surface until 2mm thick. Cut pastry into 8cm rounds. Place level teaspoons of filling into centres of rounds, brush edges of

Ricotta Dumplings: Combine cheese, sifted flour and coriander in bowl, mix with hand to a firm dough. Roll 2 level teaspoons of dough into an oval shape, repeat with remaining dough. Shallow-fry dumplings in hot oil until just browned; drain on absorbent paper.

■ Spinach sauce and dumplings can be made, and kept separately, a day ahead.
■ Storage: Covered, in refrigerator.
■ Freeze: Ricotta dumplings suitable.
■ Microwave: Not suitable.

FLAT POPPYSEED BREAD

60g compressed yeast
1½ cups warm water
1½ tablespoons castor sugar
⅔ cup plain yogurt
2 eggs, lightly beaten
160g ghee, melted
1 tablespoon salt
7 cups (1kg) plain flour
1½ tablespoons poppy seeds

Combine yeast, half a cup of the water and half the sugar in bowl, cover, stand in warm place about 15 minutes or until mixture is frothy.

Combine yogurt, remaining water, remaining sugar, eggs, half the ghee and salt in bowl; stir in yeast mixture. Sift flour into large bowl, stir in yogurt mixture, mix to a soft dough. Turn dough onto floured surface, knead for about 5 minutes or until smooth and elastic. Place dough into oiled bowl, cover, stand in warm place about 1 hour or until doubled in size.

Knead dough again, divide dough into 16 portions, stand 10 minutes. Pat dough into oval shapes about 12cm x 16cm. Place 2 ovals on preheated ungreased oven tray. Brush ovals with remaining ghee and sprinkle with poppy seeds. Bake in hot oven about 10 minutes or until puffed and lightly browned. Repeat with remaining ovals.

Makes 16.

■ Recipe best made just before serving.
■ Freeze: Not suitable.
■ Microwave: Not suitable.

AROMATIC RICE

2 cups (360g) basmati rice
20g ghee
2 teaspoons cumin seeds
1 cinnamon stick
6 cardamom pods
1 litre (4 cups) boiling water
pinch saffron powder
1 large vegetable stock cube

Rinse rice under cold water until water runs clear; drain. Heat ghee in pan, add seeds, cinnamon and cardamom, stir over heat until aromatic. Add rice, cook, stirring, 1 minute. Add water, saffron and crumbled stock cube, simmer, covered, about 10 minutes or until all liquid is absorbed and rice is tender. Discard cinnamon and cardamom.

■ Rice can be made a day ahead.
■ Storage: Covered, in refrigerator.
■ Freeze: Suitable.
■ Microwave: Suitable.

LEFT: Flat Poppyseed Bread, Ricotta Dumplings in Chilli Spinach Sauce.
RIGHT: Aromatic Rice.

CHICK PEA SALAD

1½ cups (280g) dried chick peas
2 medium (about 260g) tomatoes, peeled, seeded
2 small (about 340g) green cucumbers, seeded
1 small (about 80g) onion, finely chopped
1 tablespoon chopped fresh coriander
1 tablespoon chopped fresh mint
2 tablespoons chopped fresh lemon grass

DRESSING
¼ cup lime juice
2 teaspoons oil
1 clove garlic, crushed
2 teaspoons grated fresh ginger
1 small fresh red chilli, finely chopped
1 teaspoon sugar

Cover peas well with water in bowl, cover, stand overnight.

Drain peas, rinse, place in pan, cover with water, simmer, covered, about 1 hour or until peas are just tender. Drain, rinse under cold water; drain, cool.

Combine peas with chopped tomatoes, chopped cucumbers, remaining ingredients and dressing; mix well.

Dressing: Combine all ingredients in jar; shake well.

■ Chick peas can be cooked 2 days ahead. Salad can be made a day ahead.
■ Storage: Covered, in refrigerator.
■ Freeze: Not suitable.
■ Microwave: Not suitable.

CORIANDER DHAL

1 cup (about 200g) brown lentils
½ cup red lentils
1 tablespoon oil
1 teaspoon cumin seeds
1 teaspoon yellow mustard seeds
½ teaspoon garam masala
1 clove garlic, crushed
1 teaspoon grated fresh ginger
¼ cup chopped fresh coriander
2 teaspoons lime juice
1 medium (about 130g) tomato, seeded, chopped

Add brown lentils to pan of boiling water, boil, uncovered, 7 minutes. Add red lentils, boil, uncovered, 10 minutes; drain. Heat oil in pan, add seeds, garam masala, garlic and ginger, cook, stirring, until aromatic. Stir in lentils, coriander, juice and tomato, cool, cover, refrigerate several hours or overnight.

- Recipe can be made a day ahead.
- Storage: Covered, in refrigerator.
- Freeze: Not suitable.
- Microwave: Not suitable.

MANGO CHUTNEY

4 medium (about 1.7kg) under-ripe mangoes
1 tablespoon coarse cooking salt
1 cup water
⅔ cup cider vinegar
1 cup castor sugar
1½ teaspoons grated fresh ginger
1 clove garlic, crushed
1 cinnamon stick
2 tablespoons raisins, chopped
pinch chilli powder

Cut mangoes into strips lengthways. Combine mangoes with salt and water, cover, stand overnight.

Drain mangoes; discard liquid. Combine vinegar and sugar in pan, bring to boil. Add mangoes with remaining ingredients. Simmer mixture, uncovered, about 45 minutes or until mixture thickens, stirring occasionally. Discard cinnamon. Spoon chutney into hot sterilised jars; seal while hot.

Makes about 3 cups.

- Recipe best made 2 weeks ahead.
- Storage: Cool, dry place.
- Freeze: Not suitable.
- Microwave: Not suitable.

CUCUMBER RAITA

1 small (about 170g) green cucumber, peeled, seeded
1⅓ cups plain yogurt
1 medium (about 150g) onion, finely chopped
1 tablespoon chopped fresh mint

Combine chopped cucumber with remaining ingredients in bowl; mix well.

- Recipe best made just before serving.
- Freeze: Not suitable.

LEFT: Chick Pea Salad.
ABOVE: Clockwise from left: Mango Chutney, Cucumber Raita and Coriander Dhal.

DATE SYRUP PANCAKES

1½ cups self-raising flour
½ cup plain flour
½ teaspoon ground cardamom
½ teaspoon mixed spice
1 tablespoon brown sugar
1 egg, lightly beaten
1¼ cups milk, approximately

DATE SYRUP
1 medium (about 80g) lime
3 cups (750g) castor sugar
2 cups water
3 cardamom pods, crushed
1 small stick cinnamon
250g large fresh dates, pitted, sliced

Sift flours and spices into bowl, stir in sugar. Gradually stir in egg and enough milk to form a thick batter that drops heavily from a spoon. Cover batter, refrigerate 30 minutes.

Drop ¼ cup of mixture into heated greased heavy-based pan, spread into 10cm circle. Cook until pancake is browned underneath and bubbles appear. Turn to brown other side. Repeat with remaining batter. You need 10 pancakes for this recipe. Place pancakes onto plates, pour over hot date syrup.

Date Syrup: Using vegetable peeler, peel strips of rind thinly from half the lime, cut rind into thin strips. Combine sugar and water in pan, stir over heat, without boiling, until sugar is dissolved. Add lime rind, cardamom and cinnamon to pan, simmer, uncovered, without stirring, 3 minutes. Add dates, simmer, uncovered, about 3 minutes or until mixture is slightly thickened. Discard cinnamon stick.

- ■ Pancakes best made just before serving. Date syrup can be made a day ahead.
- ■ Storage: Date syrup, covered, at room temperature.
- ■ Freeze: Not suitable.
- ■ Microwave: Not suitable.

ABOVE: Date Syrup Pancakes.

Fabrics, table and elephants from Gallery Nomad; copperware, trays and statuette from The Windsor Antique Market; Aromatic Rice pot and Ricotta Dumplings bowl from Gallery Nomad.

Smart and Simple

Serves 8

Baby Beet and Bean Salad with Rye Croutons

traminer or colombard

Blue-Eyed Cod with Caper and Herb Crust

Tartare Sauce

Straw Potatoes

Tomato and Onion Salsa

chardonnay or chenin blanc

Almond Cream and Fruit Terrine

sauternes-style sweet wine

The jewelled effect of our do-ahead dessert terrine, like all of this menu, is smart and simple. The unusual salad takes only minutes to assemble from prepared ingredients. Next, crispy fish cutlets are lightly fried then baked just before serving with straw potatoes and fresh tomato salsa; and the tartare sauce can be made well ahead. It's best to make the terrine the day before as the filling takes time to set.

BABY BEET AND BEAN SALAD WITH RYE CROUTONS

⅔ cup black-eyed beans
2 cups (300g) frozen broad
beans, thawed
60g baby mushrooms, sliced
6 bunches (about 32) baby beetroot
600g green beans
½ x 900g loaf unsliced rye bread
80g butter, melted

DRESSING
2 tablespoons balsamic vinegar
⅓ cup olive oil
2 cloves garlic, crushed
½ teaspoon grated lemon rind

Cover black-eyed beans well with water in bowl, cover, stand overnight.

Add drained black-eyed beans to pan of boiling water, boil, uncovered, about 30 minutes or until tender; drain. Boil, steam or microwave broad beans until tender; drain. Remove skins from broad beans, discard skins. Combine black-eyed beans, broad beans, mushrooms and dressing in bowl, cover, refrigerate 2 hours.

Cut off leaves about 3cm from beetroot, reserve leaves. Do not peel beetroot at this stage to prevent colour loss. Boil, steam or microwave whole beetroot until tender; drain. Cool beetroot; peel away remaining stems and skins.

Trim thick stems from reserved leaves. Boil, steam or microwave leaves until just wilted, rinse under cold water; drain. Cut green beans into 6cm lengths; boil, steam or microwave green beans until tender.

Cut bread into 1cm x 3cm pieces. Combine bread and butter in bowl, mix until bread is well coated. Place bread in single layer on oven tray, toast in moderate oven until browned and crisp, turning once.

Just before serving, drain black-eyed bean mixture; reserve dressing. Place some beetroot leaves on each plate, drizzle with some of the reserved dressing. Top with black-eyed bean mixture, green beans, beetroot and rye croutons, drizzle with remaining dressing.

Dressing: Combine all ingredients in jar; shake well.

- Black-eyed beans can be cooked 2 days ahead. Black-eyed bean mixture can be prepared a day ahead. Beetroot, green beans and croutons can be cooked a day ahead.
- Storage: Vegetables, covered, in refrigerator. Croutons, in airtight container.
- Freeze: Not suitable.
- Microwave: Broad beans and green beans, beetroot and leaves suitable.

LEFT: Baby Beet and Bean Salad with Rye Croutons.
ABOVE: Blue-Eyed Cod with Caper and Herb Crust, Tartare Sauce, Straw Potatoes and Tomato and Onion Salsa.

BLUE-EYED COD WITH CAPER AND HERB CRUST

1 cup (155g) pine nuts
¼ cup rolled oats
¼ cup sesame seeds
2 cups (200g) packaged breadcrumbs
½ teaspoon dry mustard
1 tablespoon grated lemon rind
1 tablespoon lemon juice
1 egg, lightly beaten
1 tablespoon honey
2 tablespoons chopped fresh parsley
2 tablespoons chopped fresh
lemon thyme
2 tablespoons drained capers,
chopped
1 cup grated parmesan cheese
8 blue-eyed cod cutlets
plain flour
2 eggs, lightly beaten, extra
½ cup oil

Process pine nuts, oats and seeds until finely chopped; transfer to large bowl. Stir in crumbs, mustard, rind, juice, egg, honey, herbs, capers and cheese; mix well. Toss cutlets in flour, shake away excess flour. Dip cutlets into extra eggs, then crumb mixture.

Heat oil in large pan, add cutlets in batches, cook until lightly browned on both sides; transfer cutlets to large oven tray. Bake, uncovered, in moderate oven about 15 minutes or until cutlets are tender. Serve blue-eyed cod with tartare sauce, straw potatoes and tomato and onion salsa.

- Recipe can be prepared 3 hours ahead.
- Storage: Covered, in refrigerator.
- Freeze: Not suitable.
- Microwave: Not suitable.

TARTARE SAUCE

2 egg yolks
1 egg
2 teaspoons Dijon mustard
¼ cup lime juice
2 cups oil
2 tablespoons chopped fresh parsley
2 green shallots, chopped
2 gherkins, finely chopped
2 tablespoons drained capers,
   chopped

Blend egg yolks, egg, mustard and half the juice until combined. With motor operating, pour half the oil in a slow stream into yolk mixture. With motor still operating, pour in remaining juice, then continue pouring remaining oil in a thin stream. Transfer mixture to bowl, stir in parsley, shallots, gherkins and capers; mix well.

■ Tartare sauce can be made 3 days ahead.
■ Storage: Covered, in refrigerator.
■ Freeze: Not suitable.

STRAW POTATOES

6 large (about 1.2kg) old potatoes
oil for deep-frying

Cut potatoes into 5mm slices, then into 5mm strips. Pat potato straws dry with absorbent paper.

Just before serving, deep-fry potatoes in hot oil in batches until lightly browned and crisp; drain on absorbent paper.

■ Potatoes can be prepared 3 hours ahead.
■ Storage: Covered with water.
■ Freeze: Not suitable.
■ Microwave: Not suitable.

TOMATO AND ONION SALSA

4 large (about 1kg) tomatoes, peeled,
   seeded, chopped
2 medium (about 300g) onions,
   finely chopped
1 tablespoon chopped fresh thyme
¼ cup lemon juice
1 tablespoon olive oil

Combine all ingredients in bowl; mix well.

■ Recipe can be made 3 hours ahead.
■ Freeze: Not suitable.

BELOW: Blue-Eyed Cod with Caper and Herb Crust, served with Tartare Sauce, Straw Potatoes, and Tomato and Onion Salsa. RIGHT: Almond Cream and Fruit Terrine.

China from Villeroy & Boch; cutlery from Gero; glassware from Zwiesel; table and terracotta ware from Sandy de Beyer.

ALMOND CREAM AND FRUIT TERRINE

6 egg whites
1 cup castor sugar
1½ cups (135g) coconut
1 cup (125g) packaged ground almonds
4 kiwi fruit
14 large (about 300g) strawberries
2 small bananas
12 large (about 100g) black grapes

FILLING
200g soft unsalted butter
250g packet cream cheese, softened
⅓ cup castor sugar
½ cup packaged ground almonds
2 tablespoons Amaretto

MANGO SAUCE
3 medium (about 1.3kg) mangoes, chopped
2 tablespoons lime juice
2 teaspoons Amaretto

Grease 26cm x 32cm Swiss roll pan and 15cm x 25cm loaf pan, line both with paper; grease paper. Grease 15cm x 25cm glass loaf dish (6 cup capacity).

Beat egg whites in large bowl with electric mixer until soft peaks form, gradually add sugar, beat until sugar is dissolved between additions. Fold in coconut and nuts.

Spoon three-quarters of the mixture into prepared Swiss roll pan; spoon remaining mixture into prepared loaf pan. Bake in moderately slow oven about 10 minutes or until lightly browned and firm.

Carefully turn meringue biscuits immediately from pans onto board; cool. Cut the large meringue biscuit into 3 pieces to fit base and long sides of glass dish; the meringue biscuit from the loaf pan will be used for the top of the terrine.

Place the cut pieces into glass dish with browned sides against the glass.

Spoon one-third of the filling into meringue biscuit shell, top with row of kiwi fruit, half the strawberries and row of bananas. Cover fruit with half the remaining filling. Top with remaining strawberries and grapes. Cover fruit with remaining filling. Top with remaining meringue biscuit, browned side up. Cover terrine; refrigerate several hours or overnight.

Serve sliced terrine with mango sauce.

Filling: Cream butter, cheese and sugar in small bowl with electric mixer; stir in nuts and liqueur.

Mango Sauce: Blend all ingredients until smooth; strain.

- Recipe best made a day ahead.
- Storage: Covered, in refrigerator.
- Freeze: Not suitable.
- Microwave: Not suitable.

Glossary

Here are some terms, names and alternatives to help everyone understand and use our recipes perfectly.

ALCOHOL: is optional, but gives a particular flavour. Use fruit juice or water instead, if preferred, to make up the liquid content required.
ALLSPICE: pimento in ground form.
AMARETTO: almond-flavoured liqueur.
BACON RASHERS: bacon slices.
BEEF:
Scotch fillet: eye of the rib roast; rib-eye roll; cube roll.
BEETROOT: regular round beet.
BICARBONATE OF SODA: also known as baking soda.
BOK CHOY: Chinese chard. Use leaves and young tender parts of stems. See picture below.

ABOVE: Bok Choy.

BUTTER: use salted or unsalted (also called sweet) butter; 125g is equal to 1 stick butter.
BUTTERFLY: ask your butcher to remove bone and "butterfly" or lay the meat flat.
CALVADOS: apple-flavoured brandy.
CAMPARI: made from herbs, peel of bitter oranges and quinine bark steeped in spirit.

CAPERS: pickled buds of a Mediterranean shrub used as flavouring.
CARDAMOM PODS: thin-skinned oval capsules containing about 15 seeds with a pungent spicy flavour. See picture on page 124.
CHEESE:
Australian blue: blue vein cheese.
Brie: soft mould ripened cheese.
Bocconcini: small balls of mild delicate cheese.
Feta: is white or pale cream in colour, with a soft to firm open texture and tangy, salty taste.
Goats': made with goats' milk.
Mascarpone: a fresh, unripened, smooth, triple cream cheese with a rich, sweet taste; slightly acidic.
Parmesan: sharp-tasting cheese used as a flavour accent. We prefer to use fresh parmesan cheese, although it is available finely grated.
Ricotta: a fresh, unripened light curd cheese with a rich flavour.
Soft blue vein: soft, creamy, sweet cheese with delicate blue veins.
CHICK PEAS: garbanzos.
CHILLIES: small chillies (birds' eye or bird peppers) are the hottest.
Flakes, dried: available at Asian food stores.
Powder: the Asian variety is the hottest and is made from ground chillies. It can be used as a substitute for fresh chillies in the proportion of ½ teaspoon ground chilli powder to 1 medium chopped chilli.
CHOCOLATE:
Choc Melts: are discs of dark compounded chocolate available in 375g packets; these are ideal for melting and moulding.
Dark: we used good-quality cooking chocolate.

Drinking: powdered cocoa with sugar and flavourings added.
CHOCOLATE HAZELNUT SPREAD: we used Nutella spread.
CINNAMON STICK: dried inner bark of the shoots of the cinnamon tree, see picture on page 124.
COCONUT: desiccated coconut.
Cream: available in cans and cartons.
Flaked: flaked coconut flesh.
Milk: available in cans.
Shredded: thin strips of dried coconut.
COINTREAU: orange-flavoured liqueur.
CORIANDER: also known as cilantro and Chinese parsley and is essential to many south-east Asian cuisines. Its seeds are the main ingredient of curry powder.
CORNFLOUR: cornstarch.
CORNMEAL: ground corn (maize); similar to polenta but pale yellow and finer. One can be substituted for the other but results will be slightly different.
COUSCOUS: fine cereal made from semolina.
CREAM: light pouring cream, also known as half 'n' half.
Sour: a thick commercially cultured soured cream.
Thickened (whipping): double cream or cream with more than 35 percent fat can be used.
CURRY POWDER: a convenient combination of spices in powdered form. It consists of chilli, coriander, cumin, fennel, fenugreek and turmeric in varying proportions.
EGGPLANT: aubergine.
ENDIVE: a curly-leafed vegetable, mainly used in salads.
ESSENCE: extract.
FENNEL BULB: is eaten uncooked

in salads or may be braised, steamed or stir-fried in savoury dishes. See picture below.

ABOVE: Fennel.

FILLO PASTRY: tissue-thin pastry bought chilled or frozen.

FISH SAUCE: made from the liquid drained from salted, fermented anchovies. Has a strong smell and taste; use sparingly.

FLOUR:

Rice: flour made from rice; ground rice can be substituted.

White plain: all-purpose flour.

White self-raising: substitute plain (all-purpose) flour and baking powder in the proportions of ¾ metric cup plain flour to 2 level metric teaspoons of baking powder. Sift together several times before using. If using 8oz imperial measuring cup, use 1 cup plain flour to 2 level teaspoons baking powder.

Wholemeal plain: wholewheat all-purpose flour.

Wholemeal self-raising: wholewheat self-raising flour; add baking powder to wholemeal plain (all purpose) flour as above to make wholemeal self-raising flour.

FOCACCIA: flat Italian bread.

GARAM MASALA: varied combinations of cardamom, cinnamon, cloves, coriander, cumin and nutmeg are used to make up this spice.

GHEE: a pure butter fat available in cans, it can be heated to high temperatures without burning because of the lack of salts and milk solids.

GHERKIN: cornichon.

GINGER:

Fresh, green or root ginger: scrape away outside skin and grate, chop or slice ginger as required.

Glace: fresh ginger root preserved in sugar syrup.

Ground: should not be substituted for fresh ginger in any recipe.

Pickled: vinegared ginger in shreds or paper-thin shavings.

GREEN GINGER WINE: an Australian-made alcoholic sweet wine infused with finely ground ginger.

GRAND MARNIER: orange-flavoured liqueur.

GREEN PEPPERCORNS: available in cans or jars, pickled in brine.

GREEN SHALLOTS: also known as scallions and spring onions.

HERBS: we have specified when to use fresh or dried herbs. We used dried (not ground) herbs in the proportion of 1:4 for fresh herbs; e.g, 1 teaspoon dried herbs instead of 4 teaspoons (1 tablespoon) chopped fresh herbs.

HOI SIN SAUCE: thick sweet Chinese barbecue sauce made from a mixture of salted black beans, onion and garlic.

JERSEY CARAMELS: a packaged caramel confection.

KIBBLED RYE: whole rye grains which have been cracked or broken.

KIWI FRUIT: Chinese gooseberry.

KUMARA: orange sweet potato.

LAMB:

Rack: row of cutlets.

Shank: portion of front or back leg with bone in.

LEMON GRASS: available from Asian food stores and needs to be bruised or chopped before using.

LENTILS: brown lentils are red lentils from which the seedcoat has not been removed.

LETTUCE: we use mostly cos, endive, mignonette, radicchio, coral, oak leaf, butter and rocket.

MALIBU: coconut-flavoured rum.

MARSALA: sweet fortified wine.

MARZIPAN: smooth, firm, almond-flavoured confectionery paste.

MIRIN: sweet rice wine used in Japanese cooking. Substitute 1 teaspoon sugar and 1 teaspoon dry sherry for each tablespoon mirin.

MIXED SPICE: blend of ground cinnamon, allspice and nutmeg.

MUSHROOMS:

Baby: small, unopened mushrooms with a delicate flavour.

Flat: large, soft, flat mushrooms with a rich strong flavour.

Oyster: pale, grey-white mushrooms.

Shitake: used mainly in Chinese and Japanese cooking; these can be bought either fresh or dried.

MUSSELS: must be tightly closed when bought, indicating they are alive. Before cooking, scrub the shells with a strong brush and remove the "beards". Discard any shells that do not open after cooking.

MUSTARD:

Dijon: French mustard.

Seeded: a French-style mustard with crushed mustard seeds.

Seeds: black and yellow.

OIL: polyunsaturated vegetable oil.

Macadamia nut: oil extracted from kernel of macadamia nuts.

Olive: virgin oil is obtained only from the pulp of high-grade fruit. Pure olive oil is pressed from the pulp and kernels of second grade olives. Extra virgin olive oil is the purest quality virgin oil.

OLIVE PASTE: a paste of olives, olive oil, salt, vinegar and herbs.

PANETTONE: light yeast cake with sultanas and candied peel.

PANCETTA: cured pork belly; can substitute bacon.

PAPPADAMS: made from lentils and sold in packages in different sizes.

PARSLEY, FLAT-LEAFED: also known as continental parsley or Italian parsley.

PEARL BARLEY: barley which has had most of its outer husk removed.

PEPITAS: dried pumpkin seeds.

PEPPERS: capsicum or bell peppers.

PINE NUTS: small, cream coloured, soft kernel 1 to 2 cm long.

PITTA POCKET BREAD: 2-layered flat bread; can be cut open to form a pocket.

PLUM SAUCE: a dipping sauce made of plums, sugar, chillies and spices.

POLENTA: usually made from ground corn (maize); similar to cornmeal but coarser and darker in colour. One can be substituted for the other but results will be slightly different.

PORK:

Fillet: skinless, boneless eye-fillet cut from the loin.

Loin: from pork middle.

PRAWNS: also known as shrimp.

PROSCIUTTO: uncooked, unsmoked ham cured in salt; ready to eat when bought.

PRUNES: whole dried plums.

PUMPKIN: we used several varieties; any type can be substituted for the other.

QUAIL: small game birds from about 250g to 300g.

READY-ROLLED PUFF PASTRY: frozen sheets of puff pastry available from supermarkets.

RED SPANISH ONION: large purplish-red onion.

RICE:

Arborio: large round-grained rice especially suitable for risottos.

Basmati: similar appearance to long grain rice with a fine aroma.

Brown: natural whole grain.

Puffed: grains of rice puffed under heat.

White: is hulled and polished, can be short or long grained.

Wild: from North America, but not a member of the rice family.

RICE VERMICELLI: rice noodles.

RIND: zest.

ROLLED OATS: flattened flakes of grain.

RUM: we used an underproof dark rum.

SAFFRON: available in strands or ground form. The quality varies greatly.

SAKE: Japan's favourite rice wine.

SALT:

Celery: mixture of salt and ground celery seeds.

Cooking: coarse, free-running refined salt.

Garlic: mixture of garlic powder and salt.

Onion: mixture of ground dried onions and salt.

Sea: mixture of salts produced by the evaporation of sea water.

SAMBAL OELEK (also ulek or olek): a paste made from ground chillies and salt.

SCALLOPS: we used the scallops with coral (roe) attached.

SEASONED PEPPER: a combination of black pepper, sugar and bell peppers.

SESAME OIL: made from roasted, crushed white sesame seeds. Do not use for frying.

SESAME SEEDS: there are 2 types, black and white; we used the white variety in this book.

SNOW PEAS: also known as mange tout (eat all), sugar peas or Chinese peas.

SNOW PEA SPROUTS: sprouted seeds of the snow pea.

SOY SAUCE: made from fermented soy beans. The light sauce is generally used with white meat, and the darker variety with red meat. There is a multi-purpose salt-reduced sauce available, also Japanese soy sauce.

SPATCHCOCK: small chicken weighing about 400g to 500g.

SPINACH (silverbeet): cook green leafy parts as required by recipes.

SPINACH (English): a soft-leaved vegetable, more delicate in taste than silverbeet (spinach); young silverbeet can be substituted for English spinach.

STAR ANISE: the dried star-shaped fruit of an evergreen tree. It is used sparingly in Chinese cooking and has an aniseed flavour. See picture below.

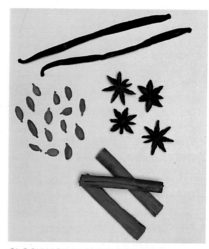

CLOCKWISE FROM TOP: Vanilla beans, star anise, cinnamon sticks, cardamom pods.

STOCK POWDER: 1 cup stock is the equivalent of 1 cup water plus 1 crumbled stock cube (or 1 teaspoon stock powder). If you prefer to make your own fresh stock, see recipes in section opposite.

SUGAR:
we used coarse granulated table sugar, also known as crystal sugar, unless otherwise specified.

Brown: a soft fine granulated sugar with molasses present.

Castor: fine granulated table sugar.

Icing: also known as confectioner's sugar or powdered sugar. We used icing sugar mixture, not pure icing sugar, unless specified.

SUGAR SNAP PEAS: small pods with small formed peas inside; they are eaten whole, cooked or uncooked.

SULTANAS: seedless white raisins.

TABASCO SAUCE: made with vinegar, hot red peppers and salt; use sparingly.

TAHINI PASTE: made from crushed sesame seeds.

TOMATO:

Paste: a concentrated tomato puree used in flavouring soups, stews, sauces, etc.

Puree: is canned, pureed tomatoes (not tomato paste). Use fresh, peeled, pureed tomatoes as a substitute, if preferred.

Sun-dried: dried tomatoes, sometimes bottled in oil.

Sun-dried tomato paste: a paste made from sun-dried tomatoes, olive oil, salt and herbs.

VANILLA BEAN: cured pod of the fruit of the vanilla orchid plant. See picture at left.

VANILLA ESSENCE: we used imitation vanilla essence.

VIENNA LOAF: oval, white, unsliced loaf of bread.

VINDALOO PASTE: thick, Indian seasoning paste with sour-hot flavour; ingredients are ground chillies, coriander, cumin, fenugreek, mustard, fennel, cinnamon and cloves in a vinegar base.

VINEGAR: we used both white and brown (malt) vinegar.

Cider: made from apples; has an acidic taste and smell.

Raspberry: made from fresh raspberries steeped in a white wine vinegar.

Red wine: vinegar made from the fermentation of red grapes.

Rice: a colourless, seasoned vinegar containing sugar and salt.

Tarragon: fresh tarragon is infused in white wine vinegar.

WASABI PASTE: green horseradish.

WINE: we used good-quality dry white and red wines.

WITLOF: also known as chicory or Belgian endive. See picture below.

ABOVE: Witlof leaves.

WORCESTERSHIRE SAUCE: is a spicy sauce used mainly on red meat.

YEAST: allow 2 teaspoons (7g) dried yeast to each 15g compressed yeast if substituting one for the other.

ZUCCHINI: courgette.

Sun-dried: dried sliced zucchini bottled in oil.

Dinner Party Planning

A dinner party is more fun if you are organised. Planning is the key. Choose a menu that suits your guests' tastes and your budget, then make lists. Foodwise, make shopping lists (one with items to buy ahead, the other with last-minute "perishables"), then plan your cooking timetable, starting with dishes which are suitable to freeze. Our recipes give helpful hints.

Wine quantities can be difficult to estimate; as a rough guide, we allow about 6 glasses per 750ml bottle.

Take stock of the "accessories" you need, as well. For a big dinner party, have you enough serving plates and china, cutlery, tables, chairs, glasses, linen and so on?

Friends and relatives can often help with china, cutlery and glasses, but it may be more convenient to hire the things you need. Shop around before hiring; we found the variations in prices quite amazing!

To make things run more smoothly at large dinner parties, consider hiring someone to serve and clean up. Many agencies provide these services, and such help is well worthwhile if your budget allows for it.

Cup and Spoon Measurements

To ensure accuracy in your recipes use the standard metric measuring equipment approved by Standards Australia:
(a) 250 millilitre cup for measuring liquids. A litre jug *(capacity 4 cups)* is also available.
(b) a graduated set of four cups – measuring 1 cup, half, third and quarter cup – for items such as flour, sugar, etc. When measuring in these fractional cups, level off at the brim.
(c) a graduated set of four spoons: tablespoon *(20 millilitre liquid capacity)*, teaspoon *(5 millilitre)*, half and quarter teaspoons. The Australian, British and American teaspoon each has 5ml capacity.

Approximate cup and spoon conversion chart

Australian	American & British
1 cup	1¼ cups
¾ cup	1 cup
⅔ cup	¾ cup
½ cup	⅔ cup
⅓ cup	½ cup
¼ cup	⅓ cup
2 tablespoons	¼ cup
1 tablespoon	4 teaspoons

We have used large eggs with an average weight of 60g each in all recipes.
ALL SPOON MEASUREMENTS ARE LEVEL.
Note: *NZ, Canada, USA and UK all use 15ml tablespoons.*

Oven Temperatures

Electric	C°	F°
Very slow	120	250
Slow	150	300
Moderately slow	160-180	325-350
Moderate	180-200	375-400
Moderately hot	210-230	425-450
Hot	240-250	475-500
Very hot	260	525-550

Gas	C°	F°
Very slow	120	250
Slow	150	300
Moderately slow	160	325
Moderate	180	350
Moderately hot	190	375
Hot	200	400
Very hot	230	450

MAKE YOUR OWN STOCK

BEEF STOCK

2kg meaty beef bones
2 onions
2 sticks celery, chopped
2 carrots, chopped
3 bay leaves
2 teaspoons black peppercorns
5 litres (20 cups) water
3 litres (12 cups) water, extra

Place bones and unpeeled chopped onions in baking dish. Bake, uncovered, in hot oven about 1 hour or until bones and onions are well browned. Transfer bones and onions to large pan, add celery, carrots, bay leaves, peppercorns and water, simmer, uncovered, 3 hours. Add extra water, simmer, uncovered, further 1 hour; strain.
Makes about 10 cups.
■ Stock can be made 4 days ahead.
■ Storage: Covered, in refrigerator.
■ Freeze: Suitable.
■ Microwave: Not suitable.

CHICKEN STOCK

2kg chicken bones
2 onions, chopped
2 sticks celery, chopped
2 carrots, chopped
3 bay leaves
2 teaspoons black peppercorns
5 litres (20 cups) water

Combine all ingredients in large pan, simmer, uncovered, 2 hours; strain.
Makes about 10 cups.
■ Stock can be made 4 days ahead.
■ Storage: Covered, in refrigerator.
■ Freeze: Suitable.
■ Microwave: Not suitable.

FISH STOCK

1½kg fish bones
3 litres (12 cups) water
1 onion, chopped
2 sticks celery, chopped
2 bay leaves
1 teaspoon black peppercorns

Combine all ingredients in large pan, simmer, uncovered, 20 minutes; strain.
Makes about 10 cups.
■ Stock can be made 4 days ahead.
■ Storage: Covered, in refrigerator.
■ Freeze: Suitable.
■ Microwave: Not suitable.

VEGETABLE STOCK

1 large carrot, chopped
1 large parsnip, chopped
2 onions, chopped
6 sticks celery, chopped
4 bay leaves
2 teaspoons black peppercorns
3 litres (12 cups) water

Combine all ingredients in large pan, simmer, uncovered, 1½ hours; strain.
Makes about 5 cups.
■ Stock can be made 4 days ahead.
■ Storage: Covered, in refrigerator.
■ Freeze: Suitable.
■ Microwave: Not suitable.

Index

TWO GREAT OFFERS FROM THE AWW HOME LIBRARY